A Systematic Guide to High Performing Teams (HPTs)

Includes Change Management Guide

By

Ken Thompson

with introduction by

Adrian Moorhouse, MBE

December 2015
Revision: 2.13

A Systematic Guide to
High Performing Teams (HPTs)

A Systematic Guide to
High Performing Teams (HPTs)

<u>A Systematic Guide to High Performing Teams (HPTs)</u>

Ken's book provides pragmatic and comprehensive models for developing high performance in teams. It is full of practical anecdotes, checklists, tips and even spreadsheets you can use to hit the ground running. I would commend it to anyone who is serious about building high performing teams in their organizations.

ADRIAN MOORHOUSE MBE, Gold Medal Winner 100-metre breaststroke, 1988 Seoul Olympics Managing Director of Lane4, Sunday Times Top 100 'Best Small Companies'

I really like the way Ken has distilled a wealth of hard won wisdom on High Performing Teams down into some deceptively easy-to-use checklists.

SIMON DODDS, Complex Adaptive System Designer, Improvement Science Coach and NHS Consultant Surgeon

I work with a number of high performance teams and find Ken Thompson's book very helpful. What I particularly like is the way I can open it anywhere and remind myself of vital aspects of team interaction.

PROFESSOR ALISTAIR FEE, Co-Founder Squid Academy

Ken Thompson continues to produce the most prescient insights on human collaboration translating techniques used by insect colonies, the most efficient bioteams in nature into practical, measurable guides. NASA listens to him. So should you.

LEON BENJAMIN, Author of Winning by Sharing and co-designer ecademy.com

A Systematic Guide to
High Performing Teams (HPTs)

A detailed review by ANDREW CROSSLEY, Management Board Member, the ServQ Alliance

The book is a practical guide for leaders and senior managers. It explains how to develop a team to its optimum efficiency and performance.

One of the main barriers to collaborative working is a lack of trust and openness, which drives a culture of low information exchange, both internally and externally, because of perceptions of confidentiality. The book promotes an integrated master framework based on analysing and improving eight key areas within two master groups of process development and change management. Ken Thompson gives detailed recommendation on four process development areas and four change management aspects together with their interrelationships and based on his extensive research and fieldwork.

To aid the reader he uses a well-structured numbered sequence of observations and recommendations. On a practical level he sets out useful tables and models for the busy manager to deploy. There is also a comprehensive Appendix giving more detail about the development and adoption of many of the models.

The book explores practical forms of professional development both individually, and in teams. For each key area there are very useful self-reflection exercises to analyse your own team's current behaviours and performance. There are then steps on how to improve the situation from the status quo to achieving better performance.

One of the best templates is an insightful 'colleague assessment' model to identify neutral, against or in favour colleagues as well as understanding the importance of their distinct influence over the team, respecting that friendship bonds are different than professional networks for a particular project.

Ken Thompson's significant experience in observing high performing, and under-performing group meetings gives the reader a good quality structure for sticking to the agenda and mapping actions. He also gives much needed advice on how to conduct virtual/telephone meetings, including the self-discipline needed to makes these more effective.

A Systematic Guide to
High Performing Teams (HPTs)

A really great analogy for effective meetings is the sterile cockpit approach used on the flight decks of planes on take-off and landing. The other practical checklist for meetings is whether key actions from previous meetings are done, on plan, at risk or missed. This is useful in a project based working environment with interdependent milestones and deadlines.

The book explores the expansion of good 'people skills' within an organisation: determining clear boundaries; the rights and duties of employees; scheduling meetings and socialising; commitment; responsibility; and critical retro-analysis of each project stage, in order to verify and mitigate potential problems as soon as possible.

Ken Thompson emphasises the importance of total transparency in the organisation, which enables a dynamic and honest workplace. He values the effort needed to understand staff, the difference between their opinions and facts, and between responsibilities and promises. Staff all living up to their promises encourages a leadership approach in all individuals and generates greater integration amongst the team. This delivers leadership and decision-making using the constructive contributions of all the team.

The book highlights three important tools: the Team Process Health Check Spreadsheet, the High Performing Teams Simulation Game and the Team Leadership Simulation Game. These tools help in the creation, analysis and control of high performance teams. The first tool is based on a spreadsheet displaying the capabilities, processes and evolution of the team through detailed and comparative charts. The last two are online simulators that help in two main areas of collaborative working.

Many of Ken Thompson's recommendation are practical steps that complement the newest standards for collaborative working including BS 11000:2010. His goal is to make an individual more collaborative in behaviour and then more open to collaborating with others for the common good, the success of the project and, in long-term, the success of the organisation as whole.

It is a concise and valuable handbook recommended for busy leaders wanting to create and sustain high performing teams.

Table of Contents

About the Authors

The book is authored by Ken Thompson who is an expert practitioner, author and speaker on collaboration, high performing teams, change management and game-based learning.

Ken has written a number of books and his work has featured in major publications including The Guardian Newspaper, Wired Magazine, The Huffington Post and The Henry Ford Magazine.

Ken has also spoken at a number of international events including TEDx, the Institute for Healthcare Improvement (IHI) and NASA conferences.

Ken is the author of The Systematic Guides series which includes:

A Systematic Guide to Game-Based Learning (GBL) in Organizational Teams, Ken Thompson, January 2016

A Systematic Guide to A Systematic Guide to Business Acumen and Leadership using Dilemmas, Ken Thompson, February 2016

A Systematic Guide to Change Management, Ken Thompson, July 2016

A Systematic Guide to Collaboration and Competition in Organizations, Ken Thompson, March 2017

All books are available on <u>Amazon</u> and make ideal delegate briefing notes for participants in game-based learning sessions by providing the underpinning theory and supporting best practice on each key topic.

Adrian Moorhouse

Ken invited Adrian Moorhouse to write an introductory chapter to the book based on his own experiences as an elite swimmer, business leader and performance coach.

Adrian enjoyed a very successful swimming career from 1978 to 1992 with numerous domestic and international successes including winning the Gold Medal in the 100-metre breaststroke for Great Britain in the 1988 Summer Olympics in Seoul.

In 1995 Adrian established Lane4, a consulting practice which helps organizations, teams and individuals to maximise their performance.

Adrian has been awarded Best Leader in The Sunday Times 100 Best Small Companies to Work For (2007 and 2009) and was listed in The Top 30 Most Influential HR Thinkers in the UK (2010 and 2011).

EXECUTIVE SUMMARY

High Performing Teams (aka HPTs) have been a consistently popular leadership and management topic for the last twenty years with dozens of excellent books published on the subject.

However, during this period, the dynamics of teams has been continuously evolving in several very significant ways including:

- Self-Managed/Collective Leadership Teams
- Cross Organizational Collaboration
- Virtual/Distributed/Mobile Teams
- Massive Teams and "virtual communities"

Many of today's teams are a hybrid of 2 or more of the above which makes them even more challenging to establish and lead. Hence the need for practical and up-to-date guidance

This guide provides a pragmatic framework for the interventions needed to successfully create and sustain High Performing Teams (HPTs) in organizations of all shapes and sizes (summarized in the diagram overleaf)

A unique aspect of this guide is that it covers and integrates <u>both individual team member change management work and the whole team process development work</u>.

The guide provides comprehensive checklists for all aspects of team process development and team member change management interventions with clear guidance and tips on when and how best to employ them.

A Systematic Guide to
High Performing Teams (HPTs)

The guide explains each of the 16 team process areas in detail and provides useful material on how to create a compelling 'Change Story' about HPTs.

AN INTEGRATED HIGH PERFORMING TEAMS MODEL

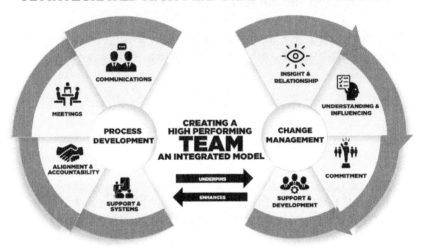

Team Change Management

The circle in the right-hand side of the model highlights the key aspects of team change management for a leader to use with the *individual members* of the team in sequence:

- Insight and Relationship
- Understanding and Influencing
- Commitment
- Support and Development

Team Process Development

The circle in the left-hand side of the model highlights 4 key team process development areas for a leader to use with the *team*. Each of these process areas can be broken down into 4 specific practices:

1: Team Meetings
- Operational Meetings
- Strategy / Problem-Solving Meetings
- Relationship / Trust Meetings
- Virtual Meeting/Phone Meeting Practices

2: Team Alignment & Accountability
- Team Ground Rules
- Team Goals & Objectives
- Team Member Accountabilities
- Team Leadership Roles

3: Team Communications
- Open Communications Practices
- Conflict Management Process
- Decision-Making Practices
- Information-sharing

4: Team Support & Systems
- Personal Development
- Coaching Relationships
- Peer Support System
- Early Warning System

A Systematic Guide to
High Performing Teams (HPTs)

Getting your team set-up, challenging though it is, is only the beginning of a team leader's journey. The guide also suggests Seven Habits of Great Team Leaders which are summarised in the diagram below to help them with the on-going leadership of the team:

7-HABITS TEAM LEADERSHIP ASSESSMENT MODEL

Copyright Ken Thompson 2015

It is important to note that any team development should always start with a "team health-check" to see which processes are the most important for the job at hand and to identify those which are totally absent or badly broken. The "one size fits all" approach to building a high performing team is seldom effective!

A Systematic Guide to
High Performing Teams (HPTs)

The guide suggests 6 key principles which can act as a practical road map for successfully creating a High Performing Team:

1. Use an existing High Performing Teams Model
2. Conduct a Team Health-Check
3. Establish Team improvement priorities
4. Build Team Maturity "Basecamps"
5. Some things take longer to fix
6. People and Process are interdependent

The guide also introduces 3 very useful support tools for HPTs – a team instant health-check calculator (free on request to readers) and online simulation game for *building* an HPT and one for *leading* an HPT.

In one appendix, 'The Team Dilemma', the guide explores the 'Me vs. We' dilemma – a challenge all leaders face concerning the tensions of being both an individual and a team member.

Finally, for team leaders in a real hurry the guide offers an approach to creating an 'Instant Team' in a morning or afternoon!

1. INTRODUCTION

By Adrian Moorhouse, MBE

We need better mental models about 'team'

Learning theorists tell us that how we react is heavily influenced by the personal 'mental models' in our heads concerning that particular situation. In simple terms, mental models link cause and effect for us. If I do A, B and C I will get X and Y. Such models are often formed subconsciously but are then continuously shaped and changed by our life experiences. If our mental models evolve in a way that makes us more successful we are said to be 'learning'. If our mental models don't evolve or flip flop in a chaotic way, we are said to be 'stuck' or 'coasting'.

The first point to remember about personal mental models is that they can never be 'correct' or 'incorrect'. This is the wrong question! The right question about any mental model is - is it useful or limiting? As Einstein allegedly once said 'All models are wrong but some are useful'.

For example, in the world of elite sports there is a mantra 'Many Inputs – One Output' which means that it is essential that a performer has a useful mental model about how the different inputs such as practice, technique refinement, nutrition, physiotherapy, study and psychological work contribute towards the goal of a winning performance. Absence of such a mental model might mean that key inputs get neglected or trivialised in the athlete's mind because the athlete cannot connect that particular input to the desired output.

The second point about personal mental models is that there are two types – explicit models and implicit models.

An explicit mental model is the answer you would give to the question 'what would you do in this situation'? An implicit mental model is what you would actually do if that situation arose. Until we have actually experienced a situation it is common for our explicit and implicit mental models to be different.

A good example is what would you do if you are driving your car and you suddenly come upon a stretch of black ice and your car starts to skid. You would probably have been taught that you should resist the temptation to turn out of the skid or apply your brakes. That would be your explicit mental model – the answer you would give to the question at a dinner party! However, your explicit mental model is no guarantee of how you would behave if you meet this situation. This is controlled by your implicit mental model. Wherever an explicit mental model is in any way counter-intuitive then it is highly likely that under stress you will not follow it.

Therefore, to be a top performer in nurturing and leading teams you need to develop, practice and refine your mental models which is really what this book is all about.

What shaped my thinking on team

My personal mental models on team have been shaped by my experiences, friends, colleagues, coaches, successes and failures in two specific communities. The first community was the elite swimming squads and teams at a club and country level from 1978 to 1992. This first community was characterised by talented, driven individuals, brutal training regimes, extensive coaching and personal development, intense competition and a constant edge about pushing your personal limits. Perhaps, surprisingly, it is also where I had some of my best experiences of being part of a team, where I had the most honest conversations and the best sense of 'having each other's backs'.

The second community was the start-up and growth of a business performance consultancy (Lane4) from 1995 to the present day. The Lane4 community was, and still is, characterised by a 'can do' attitude, entrepreneurial spirit, determination to create something of quality plus a good old fashioned hard work ethic. Working with such a supportive, learning group of people who all wanted to be there really shaped and rounded my beliefs about the essence of team.

My beliefs about High Performing Teams

So what are the absolute essentials of what makes a great team?

My implicit mental model of teams based on experience from these two very different communities suggests to me that there are 4 really critical things.

Firstly, a team needs shared values – you could call this *Team Mind*. Secondly team members need to be in real and healthy relationships with each other – *Team Emotion*. Thirdly there needs to be collective *Team Leadership* which goes far beyond the idea of a single team leader. Finally, there needs to be *Team Edge* where the team have the requisite psychological toughness to keep delivering under pressure and to bounce back quickly from set-backs.

I will try and add some colour to each of these team aspects with some real examples:

Team Mind

When we set up Lane4 we made a point of really exploring the question 'What would make this a magical place to be for you personally'? I don't just mean going around the room and writing bullet points on a flip-chart but getting into real 'one on one' and group conversations about what would stop that happening for individuals. This was not easy and took up much more time than we all would have liked. However, we made it personal and we succeeded in connecting the work to be done peoples personal ambitions and consequently their energies.

We also spent a huge amount of time discussing our values and challenging ourselves to give concrete examples of where we had lived our values in the last 3 months.... and also where we had let ourselves down! Once you have developed a strong shared set of values it makes recruitment so much easier – I have lost track of the number of times in recruitment we rejected the best candidate on paper because values did not quite align. The vast majority of these decisions turned out well.

Two of our values are Quality and Care. Recently I was humbled when a client took me aside to tell me how impressed they were by the fact that Lane4 staff always cleared up the client conference room (and the cups) after the 'big meeting' was over. Often your values are shown more in the small things you do rather than the big things. This resonates with the 'broken window' theory popularised by Malcolm Gladwell. The evidence is if a housing estate starts to get slightly run down (e.g. broken windows) it sends a subliminal message that nobody cares anymore and it can be the trigger for the start of a very rapid deterioration.

Team Emotion

It is important that there are honest and healthy peer relationships between team members. One of the weakest teams is a 'star team' where the main relationships are between the leader and the team members and the peer-peer relationships are lightweight or toxic.

I strongly believe team members need to 'contract' with each other about what each party needs from the other. As a personal example of this I remember a scenario with 4 swimmers waiting in the 'ready room' for an Olympic team relay final. Two of the swimmers had extroversion tendencies and needed to talk and two of the swimmers were more introverted and needed to be quiet and in their own worlds. You can guess what happened! Each extrovert started a conversation with an introvert. This destroyed their preparation and caused an argument in the team. When the team left the room they had lost their social cohesion which contributed to a very disappointing result in the pool. All because we did not take the time to contract with each other about our personal preparation needs.

The other key aspect of Team Emotion is creating a 'No fear' culture where people can give and receive feedback. This book strongly reinforces the importance of this and also suggests practical techniques for creating a safe environment for open communications within a team.

Team Leadership

Too often when people talk about Team Leadership they are really just talking about Team Leader. In one of Ken's earlier books on team (Bioteams) he demonstrates that the concept of a single team leader is not one that is found extensively in nature. The classic example is how geese are known to rotate the leadership role on a long migration. This idea is known as Collective or Shared Leadership.

I am not saying teams do not need leaders - of course they do! However often the best leaders are not the micro-managers but those who draw upon the leadership skills of the whole team as and when required. Such leaders are great coaches too!

The book has a strong section on team coaching and one of the principles which resonates with me is that coach and coachee are both on a learning journey. My best coaching experiences have been with two swimming coaches who were honest enough to tell me what they needed to learn to help me be successful. One-way coaching is not going to produce high performance – you need a symbiotic relationship with a coach where you are both learning together.

The idea that a coach has little to learn is a dangerous but popular misconceptions about coaching. Another popular misconception is that coaching is mostly about learning and having the coachee 'be all they can be'.

In elite sports a successful coach must be willing to constantly challenge the performer to attain ever stretching personal targets and to make many painful sacrifices along the way. Likewise, good business coaches need to have an explicit agenda which is to help the individuals achieve the targets needed from them by the organisation or team. To hit these targets there need to be regular, challenging conversations about the gaps between the individual's current performance and their targets and what they are going to do to close them. Coaching is never an end in itself!

A third popular misconception about coaching is that the coach needs to be an 'expert' in the discipline or function they are coaching. However, in the world of elite and professional sports the coaches of teams or individuals have rarely achieved the same level of aspiration as the players/performers they are coaching.

So what do coaches need to be expert in if it is not the discipline or the function?

Coaches need to be experts in leadership and need to let go of trying to be functional experts. If they cannot let go their coaching will be limited to passing on tips or experience, which might be helpful or not. This kind of coaching is not going to help performers achieve their full potential and hit demanding key organisational goals.

To take another sports analogy: whilst you may see many 'player-managers' in the lower soccer leagues you will rarely see them in the premier league. This is because the top coaches realise that they need to see and work with the big picture. This is just not possible if you are also on the pitch in the very heat of the action with the people you are supposed to be coaching!

So to sum up my beliefs on coaching. Coaching it is not just a key aspect of the job of team leadership – coaching is the job of team leadership!

I can also strongly endorse the idea that team leadership is for every team member not just the team leader through my experience in swimming squads. In some of these squads the leader was distant and in the vacuum the older squad members created a corrosive culture of blame and scapegoating. This was not conducive to high performance. To turn this around it took some of the younger members of the squads to stand up and be counted by starting to build a positive counter-culture which over a much longer period became the dominant culture. This kind of leadership involves risk and takes courage.

Another key aspect of leadership is rewards/recognition. I learned quickly in the swimming world that the rewards were always going to be more symbolic and reputational than financial. Now even though in business the rewards can be financial I consider it to be very weak leadership if this is the dominant kind of recognition given. How well do you recognise and reward through symbolism and reputation as well as money?

Team Edge

Team Edge is about ability to deliver again and again under pressure and to recover quickly from setbacks and failures. When psychological edge is not right it is easy to redefine success to mean the 'avoidance of failure'. Let me give you a real example. A leading athlete who had previously been very successful suddenly lost a race and then a second one. They were not used to losing so they never really had their psychological edge tested. Before the next race they suddenly developed an injury and pulled out. They came back the race after that but nobody really expected them to win given the injury. Can you see what is happening? They have, possibly subconsciously, redefined success and reset others expectations of them. They lost their confidence about success and high performance so they moved the goalposts to protect their reputation and self-esteem. A team with edge will recognise when they have started to shoot for booby prizes!

The final thing I would add under Edge is 'Accountability' which comes across very strongly in the book. When I was in the University of California Berkeley swim team we had a coach who each Friday afternoon asked us to share with the whole group our answers to 3 simple questions:

1. Your specific goal as a swimmer for the next week
2. Your specific goal as student for the next week
3. What you were working on to contribute as a team member

The coach would then get them typed up and the commitments of the whole squad would be given back to us first thing Monday morning to get the week off to a great start. Unless you and your team members are prepared to be publicly accountable to each other then you are unlikely to achieve High Performance.

So why read this book?

If you need to create and nurture teams which are high-performing in your organization, then you need to form effective personal mental models about what this involves. This book provides you with comprehensive practical models which you can try out, refine and make your own.

In addition to the model I have briefly outlined here, which mostly views teams through the lens of performance outcomes, the book offers two integrated 'how-to' models using the lenses of performance inputs. The book's models are totally complementary with outcomes model and in fact both are essential tools in a team leader's repertoire of high performing team models. Whereas one model comes from the 'Why and What' perspective the others complete the picture with the vital 'Who, How and When' perspectives.

The first model in this book views the creation of a high performing team as a *change management project* where the different individuals team members need to be listened to and worked with to have them 'buy in' to the concept of being a member of this high performing team and to personalise exactly what that means for them.

The second model views the creation of a high performing team as a *process/practice development project* where new disciplines need to be put in place and practiced by the team members individually, peer-peer and as a team.

It is not an 'either/or' choice! You can't build a successful team only using the models which feel more natural to you. An effective team builder/leader needs to use all the models, output models and input models, change management and process development, at the same time in an integrated way. That's what makes the job so challenging and rewarding!

Ken's book provides pragmatic and comprehensive models for developing high performance in teams. It is full of practical anecdotes, checklists, tips and even spreadsheets you can use to hit the ground running. I would commend it to anyone who is serious about building high performing teams in their organizations.

Adrian

May 2016, London

2. FRAMING HIGH PERFORMING TEAMS

High Performing Teams (aka HPTs) have been a consistently popular leadership and management topic for the last twenty years with dozens of excellent books published on the subject.

However, during this period, the dynamics of teams has been continuously evolving in a number of very significant ways including:

- *Self-Managed/Collective Leadership Teams* where the leadership role is distributed beyond a single team member
- *Cross Organizational Collaboration* where different disciplines or functions within the organization and/or different organizations participate in a single team
- *Virtual/Distributed/Mobile Teams* where at least some (sometimes all) team members are not co-located for meetings and day-to-day team operations
- *Massive Teams* often enabled by social technologies such as LinkedIn or Facebook where hundreds and thousands of individuals work (or learn) around broadly common goals within "virtual communities"

Many of today's teams are a hybrid of 2 or more of the above.

My books on teams (*Bioteams* [A3, A9] and *The Networked Enterprise* [A10]) were written to specifically address how to create HPTs in an environment where these new dynamics are present.

However, despite the abundance of books about teams (see section 6.2 for my favourite books on HPTs), I am still constantly asked whether I know of a simple practical "how to" guide that a leader or a manager can just pick up (without having to study a book) and immediately start using to establish and nurture HPTs in their own organizations.

My answer, until recently, has been, "Sadly not!" However, the question seems to keep being asked, so this short book is my attempt to provide a better answer in the form of a simple practical guide for leaders and managers who wish to nurture HPTs in their work places.

To enable us to look at what is involved in creating an HPT, there is a really important framing question we first need to consider:

Q: Is the creation of an HPT a "change management" project or a "process development" project?

Answer: Yes!

To create an HPT, you need to perform "change management" work with the individual team members and "process development" work with the team as a whole. If you neglect the process development work, you will quickly undo the results of your change management work.

For example, bad team meetings will rapidly drain any enthusiasm you have cultivated in team members through your careful change management interventions. Likewise, if you neglect the change management work with individuals, the job of creating improved team processes in isolation will be a tedious and somewhat academic exercise with no real benefits gained.

An analogy would be a racing driver (change management) and their racing car (process development). To win races, you need excellence in both the driver and the car (although it seems that great drivers racing average cars is nearly always a better proposition than average drivers racing great cars)!

It is also worth briefly touching here, whilst we are framing HPTs, on the important concept of co-evolution ("my shoes and my feet are co-evolving – they change each other.")

The change interventions and team processes you put in place should not remain static, but should change and evolve to fit together better as the team become more proficient at being an HPT.

The focus of this short book is to get you off to a solid start in terms of both change and process. It is your ongoing job of leadership to constantly refine and tweak both of these so they constantly co-evolve and improve!

3. AN INTEGRATED HPT FRAMEWORK

Below, I propose my integrated framework for HPTs which will help you identify and contextualise the main priorities for both change management [based on 10 key principles summarised in Appendix 2] and process development [based on 6 key principles summarised in Appendix 1] required to establish an HPT:

AN INTEGRATED HIGH PERFORMING TEAMS MODEL

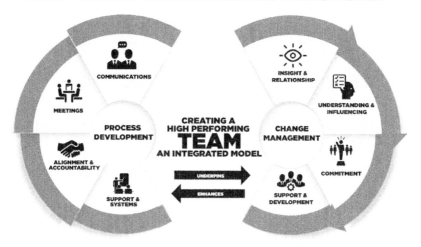

Copyright bioteams.com 2015

The model proposes 4 key team process development areas and 4 key aspects of change management with team members which we will now explore further.

3.1 Process Development for the Team

From all the research and practical experience, there are 4 areas of process which seem to be fundamental to successful HPTs:

1. Meetings
2. Alignment and Accountability
3. Communications
4. Support and Systems

These areas are of broadly equal importance and can be thought of as 4 legs of a stool – if any one of them is deficient, the stool will be unstable and not fit for purpose.

We can expand each of these areas further into 16 specific processes / practices (4 per process area):

A Systematic Guide to
High Performing Teams (HPTs)

1: TEAM MEETINGS

M1: Operational Meetings
Ensure that team operational meetings are regular and effective.

M2: Strategy / Problem-Solving Meetings
Ensure that strategy/problem solving meetings of the team are timely and effective.

M3: Relationship / Trust Meetings
Ensure that team meetings to build relationships/trust are timely and effective.

M4: Virtual Meeting/Phone Meeting Practices
Ensure that the team is able to conduct effective meetings in person or remotely/virtually.

2: TEAM ALIGNMENT & ACCOUNTABILITY

A1: Team Ground Rules
Ensure that the team has defined what constitutes acceptable and unacceptable behaviours.

A2: Team Goals & Objectives
Ensure that the team has clearly defined and communicated mutual goals and agreed how changes to these are communicated.

A3: Team Member Accountabilities
Ensure that that each team member has clearly defined accountabilities within the team.

A4: Team Leadership Roles
Ensure that, in addition to the team leader, the team enables supporting team leadership roles.

3: TEAM COMMUNICATIONS

C1: Open Communications Practices
Ensure that team members have an environment for openness with the team leader and their colleagues.

C2: Conflict Resolution Process
Ensure the team has processes to address interpersonal conflict quickly and effectively.

C3: Decision-Making Practices
Ensure the team uses recognised decision making techniques appropriate to different situations.

C4: Information-sharing
Ensure that the team effectively shares accountabilities, priorities, updates and information.

4: TEAM SUPPORT & SYSTEMS

S1: Personal Development
Ensure personal development is in place for team members.

S2: Coaching Relationships
Ensure team leader(s) are regularly in coaching conversations with other team members.

S3: Peer Support System
Ensure team members directly support and help each through collaboration.

S4: Early Warning System
Ensure team members keep a lookout for any risks which might impact other-team member's ability to deliver their results.

There are 2 very important questions you need to address before you start attempting to implement these processes in a team:

Q1: How do you establish which processes are the most important for your HPT?

Q2: Are the process priorities the same for all HPTs?

Let me start with the second question first. All teams start in a different place of capability with respect to this team process framework. Your first job as a team leader/team builder is to conduct a team process "health check" of your team against the HPT process framework. This will establish, for each of the 16 processes, whether an existing process exists, to what extent is it being used and to what extent it is working. In section 5, I will share a useful free tool which can help you conduct such a health check.

So, as all teams start in with a different process capability profile, you should generally prioritise those processes which are either absent or broken before you try to improve those which are in already place and working to varying degrees.

However, this is not the whole story as some team processes are more important than others. For example, if a regular team operational meeting is badly broken, this will damage a team every single week. Whereas, if a team relationship meeting is broken, this might only damage a team once a month or once a quarter.

It is useful to group your team processes into 3 levels of team importance/maturity with the suggestion that you address the level 1 process issues <u>before</u> you address the level 2 process issues and so on.

LEVEL 3
Advanced Processes (7)

LEVEL 2
Key Processes (5)

LEVEL 1
Foundation Processes (4)

This will allow you to create "basecamps" of process maturity as you climb the HPT "mountain" and is good change management practice which you neglect at the risk of creating "improvement chaos" within your team.

In the diagram on the next page, I suggest a practical sequence for improving the 16 team processes. Please bear in mind this is not intended to be prescriptive, but rather a guide.

For example, I suggest that, all else being equal, the 4 most important team processes to fix first are team operational meetings, team ground rules, open communications, and peer support system.

A Systematic Guide to
High Performing Teams (HPTs)

	>> LEVEL 1 >>	>> LEVEL 2 >>	>> LEVEL 3 >>
MEETINGS	Operational Meetings		
			Strategy/Problem-Solving Meetings
			Relationship/Trust Meetings
		Virtual/Phone Meeting Practices	
ALIGNMENT	Team Ground Rules		
		Team Goals & Objectives	
		Team Member Accountabilities	
			Team Leadership Roles
COMMS	Open Communications		
		Conflict Resolution Process	
			Decision-Making Practices
			Information-sharing
SUPPORT			Personal Development
		Coaching Relationships	
	Peer Support System		
			Early Warning System

SUMMARY

In team process development, you should first conduct a process health check on your team. Then, consider relative process importance to produce a process development plan for your team which is both appropriate to your team and reflective of best practice.

3.2 Change Management for the Team Members

In this section we are going to review 2 key aspects of Change Management – the Story of the Change and Change Techniques which can help bring about the Change through the individuals. **In this context, of course, the change project is the introduction of HPTs but the guidance in this section applies more generally also.**

However, BEFORE we do this it is worth briefly touching on 3 different metaphors or <u>lenses</u> for change each which can help our thinking as we develop change strategies and plans.

LENS 1: New Habits Model

In this model we say that the ultimate goal of any change is to have a group of individuals learn a set of new practices which become so deeply ingrained they become new habits. This model helps us focus on what these new habits need to be and also which old habits will need to be 'unlearned'. This allows us to work backwards from the New Habits, to the New Behaviours, to the New Practices and to the New Mind-sets.

LENS 2: Infection Model

In this model we think of change as a biological infection or disease. This can help us think of the 'places in the organizational body' which would be most vulnerable to the infection. It can also help us think about different strategies for spreading the infection such as 'word of mouth' or champions. A downside of this model is the negative connotation of an organizational disease. This can be addressed by thinking instead of an 'Antidote' model however you need to be careful that this does not dilute its usefulness as a change thinking tool.

LENS 3: Five Stages of Grief Model

The model was introduced by psychiatrist Elisabeth Kübler-Ross in her book, On Death and Dying, and was inspired by studying attitudes of terminally ill patients to their death.

The five stages, popularly known by the acronym DABDA, are:

1. DENIAL
2. ANGER
3. BARGAINING
4. DEPRESSION
5. ACCEPTANCE

The 5 stages in this grief model can be used or suitably adapted for change management – for example:

1. AWARENESS
2. CONSIDERATION
3. EXPERIMENTATION
4. ADOPTION
5. COMMITMENT

Unlike death, however at any of these stages an individual can permanently REJECT the change altogether!

This model can be used to assess what percentage of the target community are at each stage with respect to the proposed change. It can also very powerfully identify 'The Chasm' which represents the challenge of getting those individuals who are neither 'Visionaries' nor 'Early Adopters' to embrace the change ('Early Majority', 'Late Majority' and 'Laggards').

Application of the Stages model and development of effective Chasm-Crossing Strategies is explained in detail in Geoffrey Moore's 1998 ground-breaking book 'Crossing the Chasm'.

THE STORY OF THE CHANGE

Now we need to start by creating a *compelling change story* otherwise we will have no context and no possibility of real engagement. A different *chasm* metaphor can be helpful here.

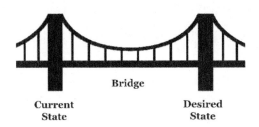

Bridge

Current
State

Desired
State

On the one side of the chasm we have the <u>Current State</u>; on the other side of the chasm we have the <u>Desired State</u>. Between these two we have the <u>Change Project</u> which is the bridge between them.

Let's look at the two sides of the chasm first.

For a change project to have any chance of success one of two situations needs to exist. Either the Current State must be unbearable or the Desired State must be very attractive. The best situation is where both conditions are part of the change story.

Change projects where the Current State is unbearable are often known as 'Burning Platform' projects in contrast to situations where unless there is change a 'Golden Opportunity' will be missed.

It is generally accepted wisdom in the change management community that 'Burning Platform' change stories tend to have more chance of success than 'Golden Opportunity' change stories. One reason for this may be because Safety and Security are more fundamental needs than Esteem and Self-actualization according to *Maslow's Hierarchy of Needs*.

Maslow's Hierarchy of Needs

5- Self-Actualization
4 - Esteem
3 - Love/Belonging
2 - Safety and Security
1 - Physiological

In developing your change story, you need to think through and 'road test' answers which will stand up to robust challenge by the toughest sceptics in your organization who will question:

- Why do we need to change?
- What is the reason for the change (Burning Platform and/or Golden Opportunity)?
- Why do we need to change now when we did not need to change before?
- Why can't we defer this change till next year?
- Who decided we need to change anyway?
- What is the hard measurable evidence for change?

- Do all our leaders believe this change is essential?
- Have we fully examined the consequences of not changing?
- Has anyone else successfully made this change yet?

This brings us on to the bridge over the chasm – i.e. the Change Project to take us from the Current State to the Desired State. Your colleagues will need to hear convincing answers about the 'how' of change and sceptics will ask hard questions such as:

- Have we a realistic change plan?
- Have we the appetite to see the change through?
- Can we afford the money and resources to do the job properly at this point in time?
- Have we learned from our previous change failures?
- What is the risk we might just make things even worse?

I share with you overleaf a checklist which I call "The 9 Cs of Successful Change Planning."

Each C defines a critical aspect of a change plan in a couple of lines.

Please note that the 9C's does not constitute your actual change plan –it is simply a check whether your change plan is covering all the key areas.

You will still need to develop a realistic change plan which is appropriately detailed for the scale of change envisaged!

A Systematic Guide to
High Performing Teams (HPTs)

Change Planning Checklist

1. Campaign
What is the end result which must be achieved by when?

2. Context:
Why is this project so important now?

3. Community
Who are the key players who are tasked with achieving this result, in other words the core team?

4. Conclusions
What are the major conclusions (or even better 'transformations') which need to be achieved to deliver the overall results required?

5. Critical Indicators
What are the critical indicators which will give you early warning of problems (*Leading Indicators*) AND ultimate measures of success or failure (*Lagging Indicators*)?

6. Constituencies
Who are the main Constituencies or interest groups who can help or hinder the achievement of the desired end result and how will they be engaged?

7. Constraints
What are the Constraints the change project must work within? These could include resources, money, skills, time or access.

8. Complications
What are the Complications which make the objectives more difficult to achieve than it would appear from the outside looking in? How will they be overcome?

9. Changes
Finally, what are the main Changes or Risks which if they happened would stop the goal being achieved and how will you mitigate against them?

CHANGE MANAGEMENT TECHNIQUES

Now we have looked at how you build a compelling and credible Story of the Change we need to look at Change Techniques for engaging the key individuals.

From research and practical experience, there are 4 aspects of team member change management which seem fundamental to successful HPTs:

1. Insight and Relationship
2. Understanding and Influencing
3. Gaining Commitment
4. Support and Development

These four aspects have an implied sequence 1 -> 2 -> 3 -> 4 to reflect 3 key change management principles namely, that you should:

- *Build rapport/relationship <u>before</u> you have serious conversations with people.*
- *Explore what people feel and want <u>before</u> you ask them to commit to anything.*
- *<u>Provide support</u> to anyone who has made a commitment to you or is struggling.*

Overleaf, I expand each of these aspects further into 9 specific interventions.

A Systematic Guide to
High Performing Teams (HPTs)

Insight & Relationships

1. Review Information about a team member.
2. Meet with a team member informally.

Understanding & Influencing

3. Seek a team member's views/advice about how well the team is working.
4. Explore what role(s) a team member might wish to play in the team.
5. Pursue feedback about issues a team member might have with you, colleagues, or team.

Commitment

6. Agree team member's accountabilities to you, colleagues and team.
7. Ask a team member to play a supporting team leadership role (formal or informal).

Support & Development

8. Help/encourage a team member to play a team leadership role.
9. Conduct a coaching/development conversation with a team member.

NOTE: *If you are using these techniques for general Change Management outside of HPTs then simply replace 'team' with proposed change' in 3 and 4, 'team leadership role' with 'champion role' in 7 and 8 and 'team member' with 'colleague' everywhere else.*

There is another very important question you must consider before you start making these interventions with your team colleagues:

Q: How do you know which intervention to make with each team member?

There are 3 things you need to determine before you chose specific change management interventions for a team member:

1. **Insight:** How well you know them and the health of your relationship?
2. **Attitude:** How they view the prospect of being in an HPT under your leadership?
3. **Influence:** How influential they are with their colleagues?

Let's look at each of these in a bit more detail:

Insight and Relationship
This is fairly obvious and relates directly to one of the 3 change management principles discussed earlier. If you lack insight or relationship, you should address this before going any further. It is said that there exists a bridge of rapport between any two individuals. If the relationship is weak, then this bridge is like a fragile wooden structure, and if it is strong, it is more like a robust concrete and steel construction. Only one of these bridges will allow 10-ton trucks to drive across it!

Attitude
You can place a person into one of three attitudes with respect to any potential future event, and HPTs are no exception. Are they <u>for</u> it, are they <u>against</u> it or are they <u>neither</u> for nor against it!

In other words, are they *Supporters, Opponents* or *Neutrals?*

You need to make sure you don't confuse a relationship issue between them and you with their attitude to the HPT. It is possible for a colleague to have a poor relationship with you and be a supporter of the HPT proposal. Likewise, a colleague you get on with really well could be an opponent of the HPT proposition!

Influence
Best practice in change management suggests firstly that you should build your change around your *high influence supporters* who can become your *champions* and influence others. Secondly, you should not worry too much initially about *opponents* unless they are *high influence opponents,* who if not carefully engaged with, could turn into *saboteurs* and derail your plans. Finally, *neutrals* will be influenced by the early adopters (and detractors). So, if you build strong momentum with the right champions, the *neutrals* and remaining *opponents* will be relatively easy to bring on board in due course.

This brings us to the important question of how do you assess an individual's influence with their colleagues?

There are two main types of influence in work situations: organizational influence and social influence.

Organizational influence depends on the person's position in the hierarchy or in a flat structure, their experience or length of service. **Social influence** depends on the person's reputation and the extent of their social network in the organization.

A Systematic Guide to
High Performing Teams (HPTs)

So, an individual with a strong reputation and a great social network could be very influential despite the fact that they might be quite junior and not the holder of one of the most senior job titles in the organization. It is important to note that they need a good reputation <u>and</u> a good social network to have social influence. A person with just one of the two could be a *secret guru* (weak network) or a *friendly lightweight* (weak reputation).

You might find the *Colleague Assessment Sheet* overleaf helpful in assessing each of your colleagues. The template helps you systematically assess Their Attitude to The Change (e.g. HPT), Your Influence on them and Their Influence on others. The first line on the template provides an example of how to complete it for a colleague.

Colleague Assessment Sheet

Summarise positions using High/Medium/Low

COLLEAGUE NAME	THEIR ATTITUDE[1]	YOUR RELATIONSHIP	YOUR INSIGHT	-> YOUR INFLUENCE	EXPERIENCE	REPUTATION	NETWORKS ->	THEIR INFLUENCE
Fred	Neutral	Low	Low	Low	High	Medium	Medium	High

1. What is their Attitude? Are they a SUPPORTER, NEUTRAL or an OPPONENT?

SOCIAL NETWORK ANALYSIS (SNA)

A very useful technique to help establish the Social
Influence of individuals is Social Network Analysis (SNA).
SNA involves constructing a map of the relationships
between every member of a group based on analysis of
their communication patterns.

SNA can be done formally by analysis of email traffic in
conjunction with one-to-one interviews with each of the
individuals in the group. You need to ask them essentially
two questions across two domains – social interactions
and work interactions:

- Who do you talk to most socially?
- Who talks to you most socially?
- Who do you go to most for information or help?
- Who comes to you most for information or help?

This information is then used to construct a 'sociogram'
which is a two-dimensional matrix summarising all the
interactions between all the individuals. The sociogram
can then be analysed, using freely available or commercial
SNA software, to reveal useful information on network
roles within the group.

Such a full analysis may be overkill for many change
management projects however it is possible to gather most
of the necessary information informally and analyse it
WITHOUT using more than a spreadsheet. For example,
there is an excellent free Microsoft Excel SNA add-in
called *NodeXL* - although basic Excel might be all you
need!

For example, you could conduct a series of 5-minute
interviews by phone and/or sit down with a few colleagues

who know the whole group well and construct a rough sociogram as a team workshop exercise.

Once you have constructed the group sociogram it is possible to analyse the network in many different ways. SNA may initially seem a bit daunting with all its different measures however there are 3 measures which can be very helpful in gaining insight about the connectivity of individuals in your group – Degrees Centrality, Betweenness and Closeness.

Degrees Centrality
Who has the most direct relationships in the network? High centrality tells you a person is well connected which is good for social influence. However, this measure does not tell you how well the person's connections are connected! They might form a closed group or clique which is not so good for social influence!

Betweenness
This dreadful term directly addresses the reality that often groups are fragmented into 2 or 3 sub-groups which are only weakly connected to each other. A person with high 'Betweenness' can be a bridge between different parts of a network which is good for social influence. However, such a person could also be bottleneck which is not so good for social influence!

Closeness
Closeness is different from Centrality and Betweenness and measures the individuals who have the best 'access' to the network as a whole taking into account their closeness or proximity to the other network members.

SUMMARY ON SNA

To sum up on Social Network Analysis within the context of Change Management:

SNA can help you understand 3 key things about a WHOLE GROUP or community:

1. Intrinsic connectivity of the whole group
How well is information flowing around the group as a whole?

2. Inter-departmental connections
How well are the different sub-groups connected to each other?

3. Informal networks
What informal teams exist across departmental boundaries?
SNA can also help you identify 3 key types of INDIVIDUALS in a group:

a. Brokers
Who are the people who act as "glue" between others?

b. Bottlenecks
Who are the people who everybody wants to talk to and are they a constraint on overall group productivity?

c. Bystanders
Who are the people who are disconnected from the group?

If you are interested in reading more about SNA there is an excellent two-part introduction to Social Network Analysis written by *Richard Cross* as a guest article on my blog at:

http://www.bioteams.com/2006/03/28/social_network_
analysis.html

Now another key question following on from this
discussion of SNA and social influence is:

*Q: Which is more powerful - organizational influence or
social influence?*

A: It depends!

In general, in well-established or large organizations
organizational influence counts for most, whereas in start-
ups, small and non-traditional enterprises social influence
can be the most important.

You will need to decide which is the more powerful
influencing dynamic in your own organization.

SUMMARY ON CHANGE MANAGEMENT

In team member change management, you need to
prioritise and make change management interventions
with your colleagues which take fully into account the
insight and relationship you have with them, their attitude
to your HPTs proposal, and how influential they will be
with their colleagues in helping drive forward (or hinder)
the change.

HOWEVER, before you do any of this this you will have
had to build up a compelling and robust 'Story of the HPTs
Change' which addresses both the WHY and HOW
questions.

4. TEAM PROCESS DEVELOPMENT: THE DETAILS

4.1. Team Meetings

It has been said that meetings take minutes but waste hours!

Here are 4 processes, which if properly implemented, will transform your team meetings:

M1: Operational Meetings

Good operational meetings, whether co-located or virtual, are the engine of organizational and project governance. However, often their success is left totally to chance.

Here are my 5 key tips for making your team operational meetings more effective:

1. Sterile Cockpit - Maintain Focus!

Sterile Cockpit is an aviation term which means that during critical phases of flight, such as take-off and landings, nothing else should be discussed by the flight crew apart from the take-off or landing. *Even if it is important,* the crew must keep it for later.

In operational meetings, this means stick to the agenda. No matter how interesting a new topic suddenly appears, don't get distracted if it is not directly pertinent to the main reason you are meeting.

The *FAA Sterile Cockpit* rule goes on to say the cockpit team should avoid "activities such as eating meals, engaging in nonessential conversations within the cockpit and nonessential communications between the cabin and cockpit crews, and reading publications not related to the proper conduct of the flight or not required for the safe operation of the aircraft." So, reading your blackberry email during an important meeting violates Sterile Cockpit.

2. Jackanory - No Story-telling i.e. reasons, explanations, justifications, causes....

Jackanory is Cockney rhyming slang for 'Telling a Story.' When we tell a story about why something has occurred, we usually, without realising it, begin to defend and justify. This wastes time and energy. Instead of telling a story, we should practice only giving the absolute minimum facts to allow the meeting to determine the correct action. The time for stories is after the meeting in the bar!

3. Sherlock Holmes - Reveal rather than conceal!
Sherlock Holmes was a famous, but fictitious detective who had a fantastic ability to uncover the truth in difficult circumstances. A team should not expect their team leaders to have the same level of investigative and deductive skills as Sherlock. Team members must make it easy for the leader of the meeting to find the information they need. So put it right out there without needing to be interrogated!

"Once you eliminate the impossible, whatever remains, no matter how improbable, must be the truth." Arthur Conan Doyle, creator of Sherlock Holmes, 1859-1930

4. Only Four Task States - Done, On Plan, At Risk and Missed

Ultimately, there are only 4 states a particular task or activity may be in. The sooner you can allocate the state to the task, the sooner you can decide what actions, if any, need to be taken.

Done or On Plan
Just say "well done" - no further discussion is necessary in the meeting. Of course, you and the rest of the team can challenge this statement if you disagree or need more evidence!

At Risk or Missed
A new commitment is needed; help may be required from the rest of the team. The team needs to be happy that any new commitment is one they can rely on given the previous one did not deliver. Commitments are described in more detail in the TEAM ALIGNMENT & ACCOUNTABILITIES section.

*5. Five Key Meeting Roles - Customer, Facilitator,
Timekeeper, Scribe and Sensor*

Meetings tend to be much more successful if the following
roles (or equivalent) are allocated to participants before
the meeting starts.

Normally the main team leader and facilitator will allocate
these roles as appropriate:

Customer
The person who, given their role, has the biggest need for
the meeting to produce a successful outcome. Being the
meeting customer, they decide if they are satisfied with the
meeting. This is usually the main team leader but not
always.

Facilitator
Generally steers and oils the running of the meeting and
makes sure it follows the tips described above. Also makes
sure the customer gets what they need (sometimes in spite
of the customer).

Timekeeper
Ensures that the meeting always knows where it stands
with respect to time so that it allocates/reallocates
appropriate time to items in a sensible way.

Scribe
Takes notes during the meeting and produces
actions/notes afterwards.

Sensor

The objective is having somebody 'sense' the temperature of the meeting and to spot unhelpful group moods. For example, resignation or complaint. This role is sometimes also played by the Facilitator.

Self-Reflection on your Operational Meetings

- To what degree are the operational meetings of your team regular and effective - *Largely, Partially or Not at all?*
- What is the best thing about your Operational Meetings and how could this be really developed and extended?
- What is the **one thing** about your Operational Meetings that is missing or could be done differently?

M2: Strategy / Problem-Solving Meetings

To successfully conduct a strategy or problem-solving meeting, the team first need to sharply define and clarify the purpose of the meeting and then employ a suitable technique to help them achieve their goal.

Two very useful techniques in this context are Brainstorming and the "5 Whys."

Let us briefly look at each in turn starting with Brainstorming.

Brainstorming

Brainstorming, despite the popularity of the term, is one of the most challenging collaborative activities to carry out in any team. While most people think they instinctively know how to brainstorm, very few have really gotten the basic rules needed to make a brainstorming session work effectively.

For example, one of the most common mistakes is the one of criticizing or listing the reasons why an idea suggested by someone else is not good. This should be avoided at all costs, since this is a powerful turn-off for anyone.

Rather than approving or disapproving other people's ideas, it is much more important to leverage the suggestions (bad and good) of others to come up with new and more relevant ideas. So, there is no need to stop and say "excellent!" or "no, this doesn't work."

Allow all ideas to come out freely and with no censorship or judgment, as each and every one of them can serve as a spark for one of your brainstorming minds to hook up and fire the winning idea. Here some specific suggestions you can use to make your brainstorming sessions more productive:

1. Sharpen the Focus

"Start with a well-honed statement of the problem."

The more focus you have at the start of a brainstorming session, the more likely that the participants will contribute useful and relevant ideas to it. Make a special effort in clarifying beyond doubt what the objective is and what needs to be found.

2. Playful Rules

"Don't start to critique or debate. Instead encourage wild ideas."

Never criticize or put down someone else idea just because it doesn't fit your expectations. Use other people contributions to spin off new ideas and do not waste any time criticizing or explaining why someone else's idea is not good. Just keep contributing new stuff with a positive, constructive attitude.

3. Number Your Ideas

"Go for quantity - 100 ideas per hour is a good target"

The more ideas you can collect in a brainstorming session, the better. Spend time after the session to identify, single out, and number the most valuable ones. Even better, if during the brainstorming session as new ideas come up, number and note them down on a public board visible by everyone so that others can keep using and referencing them in the process.

Research shows that the best ideas tend to occur near the end of brainstorming sessions when people have exhausted the obvious.

4. Build and Jump

"When the energy starts to fade, a facilitator should build on an idea or take a jump."

If at any one point during a brainstorming session, you feel the energy and the contributions are slowing down, take the one best idea that has emerged so far and take it up for dissection, analysis and as a spin-off for more ideas.

5. The Space Remembers

"Capture the ideas in a medium visible to the whole group."

Mind-mapping and visual storyboarding of your brainstorming outputs can be tremendously effective. Especially when you can use the talent of one of your brainstormers to convert simple concepts and ideas into immediately recognizable icons or images.

6. Stretch Your Mental Muscles

"Warm up if the group are new to each other or don't regularly brainstorm or are likely to be distracted by other pressing matters."

Breaking the ice and warming up the creative spirit among brainstormers is of the essence to obtain good results. Playing some intellectual game or running a humorous competition before brainstorming can often give the right "zing" to the team that needs to focus later on new ideas.

7. Get Physical

"Encourage diagrams, stick figures (2-D), mock-ups and models (3-D)."

Visualizing new ideas is very effective. The more you can involve your body and the rest of the team in doing so as well, the more engaging and effective the results that can stem from this process.

5 Whys

The "5 Whys" technique was invented many years ago by the Total Quality and Lean Communities to ensure that the right root problem is being solved and not just one of its symptoms.

It is described in many places on the web which you can google, and which I won't duplicate here except to offer a short summary of how to use "5 Whys" based on guidance from the UK National Health Service.

How to complete the 5 whys:

1. Write down the specific problem. Writing it down helps you formalise the problem and describe it accurately. It also helps a team focus on the same problem.

2. Use brainstorming to ask why the problem occurs then, write the answer down below.

3. If this answer doesn't identify the source of the problem, ask 'why?' again and write that answer down.

4. Loop back to step 3 until the team agrees that they have identified the problem's root cause. Again, this may take fewer or more than '5 whys?'

If you are leading strategy/problem-solving meetings with large groups made up of participants with very different interests or participants who do not really know each other then please check out my 'Egoless Meetings' approach described in Chapter 10.

Self-Reflection on your Strategy / Problem-Solving Meetings

- To what degree are the strategy/problem solving meetings of your team timely and effective - *Largely, Partially or Not at all?*
- What is the best thing about your Strategy / Problem-Solving Meetings and how could this be really developed and extended?
- What is the **one thing** about your Strategy / Problem-Solving Meetings that is missing or could be done differently?

M3: Relationship / Trust Meetings:

It is amazing how many teams leave relationship building meetings to chance or expect all the relationship and trust building to be achieved through a pizza, ten-pin bowling or even a team-building exercise. These things are good in themselves, so please don't stop them, but they are not what I mean by a team relationship/trust meeting.

Like anything else, if you wish to build relationship and trust, then you must make it the primary objective of a team meeting and not a hoped-for by product which results from focussing on some other objective.

To build trust and relationship, you need to systematically apply the 4 disciplines of individual change management mentioned earlier in section 3.2. The difference is that you need to apply them *to the team as a* whole – moving from one-to-one to many-to-many.

So, to develop team relationships and trust you need to:

1. *Develop* Insight and Relationship between colleagues
2. *Understand* what makes colleagues tick
3. *Grow* Commitment between colleagues
4. *Support* and Develop each other

To achieve this there are a number of techniques you can employ as a team including:

- Getting to know colleagues as people outside work
- Giving and receiving 360-degree feedback
- Sharing ambitions and concerns
- Seeking and offering help with day to day issues
- Celebrating success (and commiserating failures)

However, for most of these techniques to be effective, the team will have to develop its skills and sensitivities in Open Communications which is described in more detail in the Team Communications section.

It is also vitally important as a team leader that, as well as internal team relationships, you also foster positive relationships between your team and other teams.
For more details on inter-team see Chapter 11.

Self-Reflection on your Relationship / Trust Meetings

- To what degree are the team meetings to build your relationships/trust timely and effective - *Largely, Partially or Not at all?*
- What is the best thing about your Relationship / Trust Meetings and how could this be really developed and extended?
- What is the **one thing** about your Relationship / Trust Meetings that is missing or could be done differently?

M4: Virtual/Phone Meeting Practices:

These days, it is often a luxury for a whole team to be able to meet together in the same room. Thus, the growth in virtual meetings where not all the participants are co-located during the meeting.

Virtual meeting technologies have advanced rapidly with video conferencing and screen-sharing technologies where control can be switched between remote presenters. However, the most widely used tool for virtual teams is still the plain old telephone conference call. Sadly, it is also the most badly used!

So, whether you are talking over Skype, mixing it with screen sharing and messaging, using your corporate PABX, or just calling in to an external service, if you follow these 12 simple rules you will get much better virtual meetings.

1. *Pick a reliable phone/web service*
It is better to pay a bit for a good meeting than to pay nothing for a meeting which does not run properly and wastes people's time. The time wasted can cost a lot more than the money saved from a free but poor service.

2. *Send out two emails*
Send the first one when the meeting is set-up, and the second one close to the scheduled call time. State the purpose of call, who is chairing it, and the call-in details.

3. *Text a reminder*
On the day of the meeting for those who did not read your email or who are on the move.

4. Arrive Early
Don't arrive fashionably late. It wastes other people's time and money. Remember that if you are the chairman, you <u>must</u> be the first person on the meeting call.

5. Keep it short
Virtual meetings should rarely run for more than an hour and never more than two. Thirty minutes or less is best. Don't overrun no matter how important it is. Reschedule. Otherwise no one will turn up at your next virtual meeting!

6. Use your landline
Only dial in on mobile phone if you have no other options.

7. Keep the noise down
Don't dial in from somewhere with background noise. Always put you phone on mute when you are not speaking to avoid transmitting background noise.

8. Limit the small talk
It is OK to use the first few minutes for people to socialise the meeting through some small talk, but this needs to be controlled as some people may be ringing in on expensive mobile cells. Meeting latecomers should simply state their names on arrival, and the chairperson should resist the temptation to bring them up to speed by summarising the meeting for them *unless absolutely essential.*

9. On Point
Keep all your contributions short and focussed, and don't ramble.

10. Don't interrupt
Make doubly sure the other person has finished speaking before you start to ensure you don't "talk-over." If in any doubt, just keep listening for a few seconds longer!

11. Manage the call
If you are the chairperson, don't let one person dominate or destroy the call for everyone else. Don't be guilty of doing this yourself either!

12. Sum-up
The chairperson should summarise the key points and send out (or delegate) a very short email summary within 24 hours.

Self-Reflection on your Virtual/Phone Meeting Practices

- To what degree are your team able to conduct effective meetings in person or remotely/virtually - *Largely, Partially or Not at all*?
- What is the best thing about your Virtual/Phone Meetings and how could this be really developed and extended?
- What is the **one thing** about your Virtual/Phone Meetings that is missing or could be done differently?

4.2. Team Alignment & Accountability

These processes address the critical team challenge of getting and keeping everyone aligned with the objectives and values of the team. Also making sure that every team member knows what they are being counted on for and what they can count on their team colleagues for.

A1: Team Ground Rules

Ground rules are the agreed position of the whole team
regarding what behaviours are expected, and what action
should be taken, if this is not the case. Ground rules should
be short, sharp, unambiguous and unanimously agreed,
otherwise they cannot be enforced. Unfortunately, most
teams either have no ground rules or have set the bar far
too high with unrealistic ground rules.

The best ground rules documents are contained on a single
page of A4 paper.

Unrealistic ground rules quickly become discredited, as
most people don't comply with them, and then it can be
very hard to put in any ground rules whatsoever. Ground
rules are worthless unless implemented and a *light* set of
ground rules which have been implemented is always
better than a *heavy* set of ground rules not implemented
or observed.

This means that any violations have to be dealt with early
on, or else the ground rules are not worth the paper they
are written on.

A Systematic Guide to
High Performing Teams (HPTs)

Here is my suggested 10-point Team Ground Rules Checklist:

1. Team Values
What **positive** behaviours/values will the team seek to embrace and exemplify?

2. Trust Damagers and Destroyers
What **negative** behaviours would damage/destroy trust in the team and how will the team avoid/deal with this?

3. Conflicts of Interest
Are there any obvious potential conflict of interest scenarios and, if so, how should they be handled?

4. Team Boundaries and Member Types
What are the boundaries of the team and the different types of team member participation (e.g., Core, Part-Time, Reviewer or Expert)?

5. Information Sharing
Where will there be transparency of information sharing and where will there be privacy and restricted sharing within the team?

6. Issue and Conflict Resolution
How will issues and conflicts be resolved, and what will be the main steps in this practice? Team conflict resolution is described in more detail in the TEAM COMMUNICATIONS section.

7. Decision-Making Practices
How will decisions be made in the main categories: Strategic: Wide Operational (affects most team members), Tactical: Narrow Operational (affects only a few team

members)? Team decision making is described in more detail in the TEAM COMMUNICATIONS section.

8. Meetings
What types of team meetings will there be? What will be their purpose, frequency, attendees and channels (e.g. face to face, phone, online)? Team Meetings are described in more detail in the TEAM MEETINGS section.

9. Induction, Mentoring and Buddying
Will the team be taking on new members and, if so, how will they be brought up to speed and by whom?

10. Communications Tools
Which tools will be used for which type of communications (urgent, important), and what will be the agreed "Reply by" times?

Please see also my R.A.P.P.O.R.T checklist in Chapter 8 for an 'express' combined set of Team Goals and Ground Rules for teams who are in a real hurry!

Self-Reflection on your Team Ground Rules
- To what degree has your team defined and agreed what constitutes acceptable and unacceptable behaviours - *Largely, Partially or Not at all*?
- What is the best thing about how you behave towards each other and how could this be really developed and extended?
- What is the **one thing** about how you behave towards each other that is missing or could be done differently?

A2: Team Goals & Objectives

It all seems pretty obvious stuff, but surprisingly the setting of team goals and objectives is often omitted or carelessly done by many teams. If you don't do this one properly, then all the rest won't matter!

Key things to be considered are:

1. Team Purpose/Objectives/Goals
What is the purpose of the team (timeless)?

2. Team Purpose/Objectives/Goals/Milestones
What are the objectives (long-term), goals (medium-term) and milestones (near-term) of the team and the specific timeframes associated with each of them?

3. Team Lifespan
Is the team to exist for a limited time only or is it on-going?

4. Team Sponsor/Stakeholders/Customer
For whose benefit has the team been created and what results do each require in terms of:

- Team Outputs/Deliverables/ Outcomes
- Team KPIs / Leading Indicators of Success

5. Team Critical Success Factors
What 3 or 4 key things must happen or be maintained for the team to succeed?

6. *Team Risks*
What are the main risks to the team's success and how will
they be mitigated against?

7. *Team SWOT*
Does the team understand its Strengths, Weaknesses,
Opportunities and Threats?

*Please see also my R.A.P.P.O.R.T checklist in Chapter 8
for an 'express' combined set of Team Goals and Ground
Rules for teams who are in a real hurry!*

Self-Reflection on your Team Goals & Objectives

- To what degree has our team clearly defined and
  communicated mutual goals and agreed how
  changes to these are communicated - *Largely,
  Partially or Not at all*?
- What is the best thing about how you deal with
  Team Goals & Objectives and how could this be
  really developed and extended?
- What is the **one thing** about how you deal with
  Team Goals & Objectives that is missing or could be
  done differently?

A3: Team Member Accountabilities

To best appreciate how to achieve team member accountability, we first need to appreciate the difference between a *promise, a responsibility* and a *guarantee.*

In the recent UK floods on the TV news, we heard a lot about defences failing and phrases being bandied about by engineers and managers such as "a once in a hundred years" event and "could never have been envisaged." However, when you hear these types of explanations, it is always interesting to listen for the commitment or lack of it in the speaker.

Often organizations, in the worthy name of professionalism, quality and standards, freely hand out **responsibilities** but neglect more valuable **commitments**.

What's the difference?

Responsibilities
For example, in the floods scenario, a responsibility is to make sure that all maintenance is fully up to date on a flood barrier. Usually, there is no shortage of people with statements such as these in their job descriptions. However, this is a million miles short of somebody making a *promise* that the barrier will not fail!

Promises vs Responsibilities
Do people in your team hold real commitments (aka promises) or just responsibilities? If they don't then the team will constantly fail ....and it will be nobody's fault (except perhaps you - the team leader)!

Does anyone in your team get held to account if the teams "flood defences" fail?

I am not talking about "the blame game," but, in fact, the vital missing ingredient in many teams' organization's governance and oversight systems!

Now promises have to be held voluntarily and willingly; they cannot be ordered or demanded. So, if someone is asked to hold a promise that the flood defence will not fail, then it is perfectly reasonable for them to say that they need to discuss and negotiate the "supports" which would need to be in place for them to be able to make this promise with confidence.

This is a really valuable conversation in any team or organization - what would need to happen or change for you to be able to a promise which is valuable but seems out of reach?

If this conversation is conducted well, it will identify changes that nobody has really thought about and even uncover major flaws in existing designs. This is because we automatically think in a totally different way about things when we feel truly accountable for the outcomes. Anticipated promises give their potential promise-holders a powerful kind of instinctive x-ray vision of what is really missing!

Guarantees
Sometimes people resist promises because they believe they are being asked to give guarantees. A promise is no more a guarantee than a responsibility is a promise!

A pilot promises to fly the passengers safely to their destination on time and will die attempting to honour this promise, but they cannot guarantee that there will always be a satisfactory outcome every single time.

The reality is however, that no matter how professional your people are and how complete their responsibilities are, unless you have gone beyond this and secured their promises, you will regularly fail to live up to your implied and explicit customer commitments.

In an HPT, there will be at least 5 different types of promises held (in fact a "network of promises"):

- Promises held by the team leader to external stakeholders
- Promises held by team members to one or more team leaders
- Promises held by supporting team leaders to the main team leader
- Promises held by team leaders to team members (typically around support and development)
- Promises held by team members to each other (typically around helping each other)

If any one of these types of promises is missing, it is unlikely the team will achieve high performance.

For a great introduction to *Commitment-Based Management (CbM)* check out Professor Donald Sull's 3-part short video series on *Youtube* entitled

"Promise based management: London Business School"

(https://www.youtube.com/watch?v=tNbU2rQuz_I)

A Systematic Guide to
High Performing Teams (HPTs)

To dig deeper into the discipline CbM I recommend the Harvard Business Review paper from the April 2007 Issue.

"Promise-Based Management: The Essence of Execution" by Donald Sull and Charles Spinosa

(https://hbr.org/2007/04/promise-based-management-the-essence-of-execution)

Self-Reflection on your Team Member Accountabilities

- To what degree has each team member clearly defined accountabilities within the team - *Largely, Partially or Not at all*?
- What is the best thing about how you deal with Team Member Accountabilities and how could this be really developed and extended?
- What is the **one thing** about how you deal with Team Member Accountabilities that is missing or could be done differently?

A4: Team Leadership Roles

One of the weakest types of teams is the one where all leadership is vested in a single individual! This is because such a team is not utilising all its collective brainpower and also it has zero fault tolerance; if the leader gets it wrong then there is no fall-back.

In my bioteams book [A9], I describe how nature's teams tend to be collectively led where the leadership role is either rotated or spread across multiple team members. This is also a principle in self-directed/self-organising teams.

In fact, bioteams takes this even further suggesting that every member of your team should be treated as a leader in at least some respect.

A bioteam is an organizational structure in which peers share power and responsibility, and each member of the team is a both a leader and a follower. The structure is modelled after a fluid leadership structure found in nature.

Therefore, an HPT should design collective leadership structures to which fully take advantage of the strengths and capabilities of all its members.

Leadership roles can be designed in a number of ways to share, for example:

- The conduct of meetings (see TEAM MEETINGS section)
- The oversight of team members
- The communications with external stakeholders and customers
- The coaching and mentoring

In bioteams, I talk about "treating every team member as a leader" and the importance of examining and reducing so-called "permission structures" within teams:

Traditional teams protect themselves against member mistakes by establishing layers of permission that must be granted before a team member may take action in certain circumstances. We call these "Permission Structures." Bioteams slash down these "Permission Structures" to the absolute bare minimum. The only permission structures kept in place by a bioteam are those needed to protect the team against the potentially critical mistakes that would threaten the sustainability of the bioteam's own mission. Accountability in bioteams is achieved through "team transparency" and "reputation-based systems", not through control and hierarchical authorization systems.

<u>Self-Reflection on your Team Leadership Roles</u>

- To what degree does your team have supporting team leadership roles in addition to the main team leader - *Largely, Partially or Not at all*?
- What is the <u>best thing</u> about how you deal with Distributed Team Leadership and how could this be really developed and extended?
- What is the **one thing** about how you deal with Distributed Team Leadership that is missing or could be done differently?

4.3. Team Communications

Team communications are the lifeblood of effective teams. Here are 4 key processes which address the way your team members communicate with each other:

C1: Open Communications Practices

Teams need an open communications process. By this, I mean teams need a safe environment where each team member can have difficult and authentic conversations with the team leaders and other team members both as a group and on a one to one basis.

To establish such safe environments, it is necessary for team members to be able to distinguish between what is an *opinion* and what is a *fact*.

A fact is something which can be verified objectively by two independent witnesses. "It rained in some parts of Belfast today (2nd December 2015)" is a fact. An opinion, however, is a subjective judgement over which two independent witnesses may disagree. "Manchester United is the best football team in England" is an opinion. Now, opinions can be given weight by associating them with facts, but this only makes them "well-grounded opinions," it never makes them facts. Facts grounding this opinion could be the number of times Manchester United has won various trophies in the last 5-10 years, their current position in the Premier League and the average number of supporters who attend their matches.

It follows that facts can be verifiably true or false. However, opinions can never be verifiably true or false; they can only be useful or not useful *to the hearer* (even if they are grounded with a multitude of facts).

Why are these distinctions so important for Team Communications?

Without these distinctions, if you try to tell me that I could have done something better or differently, then, I may listen to this as a "fact" and feel that this is a personal attack on me rather than helpful feedback. My normal reaction will also be to dispute it as a true fact and argue the opposite. However, if I understand it is only an opinion, which can never be true or false, I can choose to listen to it in a non-defensive way.

Likewise, if I am giving feedback, but unaware of these distinctions, I may try and argue and prove that I am in the right and my way of seeing is the only reasonable way of looking at the situation. This can render my feedback very hard to listen to and ultimately useless to the hearer in terms of them using it to change or improve.

This might all just seem common sense, but unless a team is trained and practiced in speaking and listening using these distinctions, then there will not be a safe and open communications environment. This means that important things which were absolutely vital for the team's success will either be left unsaid or unheard.

The Denning Institute has an excellent paper on the different between facts and opinions (which it calls assertions and assessments) which you should read:

http://denninginstitute.com/pjd/TT/AssertAssess.pdf

Assertions and *Assessments* are two types of "Speech Act" – there are 3 other types of Speech Act one of which is a *Promise* which we discussed under team Member Accountability.

Self-Reflection on your Team Communications

- To what degree does your team provide safe environments for open communications with the team leader and the other team members - *Largely, Partially or Not at all?*
- What is the best thing about your Team Communications and how could this be really developed and extended?
- What is the **one thing** about your Team Communications that is missing or could be done differently?

C2: Conflict Resolution Process

Researchers Thomas and Kilmann have identified the 5 most common ways people deal with conflict on a one to one basis:

Avoiding - "I will think about it tomorrow..."
Accommodating - "Of course I will..."
Competing - "My way or the highway..."
Collaborating - "Let's try win-win..."
Compromising - "Give a bit, take a bit ..."

That's fine on a one-to-one basis, but in a team, you need a process which is clear and agreed on to ensure it is properly dealt with in a way which takes care of all parties.

Best practice in conflict resolution within teams generally follows an escalation process along the following lines:

LEVEL 1

A point of conflict is identified between two team members which is damaging to the team and they cannot sort out themselves. At least one of the team members decides to flag it as an issue they need help with.

LEVEL 2

Both parties are encouraged to make one last attempt to resolve the issue themselves, but if they cannot....

LEVEL 3

An agreed third party (e.g. another team member) tries to help the parties reach a resolution. An important skill at this stage for the third party is to be able to determine if both parties are open to being helped in 'breaking deadlock'. If you lack this skill you can waste a lot of time just going through the motions. Here are two great questions (credit to *Stephen Covey*) which can help you determine if there is space and appetite for a negotiated solution:

Question 1:
Would you be prepared to search for a solution which is better than the one you have brought with you?

Question 2:
Are you prepared to articulate the other person's concern to their satisfaction before starting negotiation?

If you can get a YES to at least one of these questions you will have opened up a space for collaboration.

If you get two NO's you are in a situation where both sides are entrenched and no longer interested in the other party's point of view. Don't waste any more time and energy - escalate to the next level!

LEVEL 4

The issue is given to another agreed third party (e.g. a team leader) to make a decision which is then binding on both parties. Your process could be as simple as this as long as you identify how third parties become involved. It is also useful to agree a timeline for each level to avoid an issue festering away and distracting the team. You should also agree to what extent other non-impacted team members are briefed (or not) on what is happening.

Self-Reflection on your Team Conflict Resolution

- To what degree does your team have processes in place to address interpersonal conflict quickly and effectively - *Largely, Partially or Not at all*?
- What is the best thing about your Team Conflict Resolution and how could this be really developed and extended?
- What is the **one thing** about your Team Conflict Resolution that is missing or could be done differently?

85

C3: Decision-Making Practices:

"The way a team decides to decide is one of the most important decisions it makes!"

In the excellent book, "Why Teams Don't Work" [B6], the authors identify 7 key decision making styles for teams that they place in context by commenting:

"Though fashion occasionally underscores one or another of these approaches, there is no right or wrong way to decide an issue. The important thing is that the team decides, in advance, what decision-making method will be used. No surprises!"

If a team is planning to make a major decision, it should, wherever possible, discuss and agree on *how* the decision will be reached (e.g. using one of these 7 styles) <u>before</u> the actual decision making discussion starts.

At the meeting, the team leader should introduce the decision which needs to be made and then propose the decision making style which is then discussed and agreed.

1. *Consensus*
Consensus decision making is where all team members get a chance to air their opinions and must ultimately agree on the outcomes. If any team member does not agree, discussions continue. Compromise must be used so that every team member can agree with and commit to the outcomes.

2. *Majority Rule*
Majority decision making is democracy in action. The team votes, the majority wins.

3. *Minority Rule*
Minority decision making usually takes the form of a subcommittee of a larger team that investigates information and makes recommendations for action.

4. *Averaging*
Averaging is the epitome of compromise. Team members haggle, bargain, cajole, and negotiate an intentional middle position. This has been more recently referred to as the "Wisdom of Crowds" and has been shown to be most effective where specialised knowledge is <u>not</u> key to the decision.

5. *Expert*
If the team doesn't already have one in the team, find or hire an expert. Listen to what the expert says, and follow the expert's recommendations. This has been more recently referred to as the "Collective Intelligence" and has been shown to be most effective where specialised knowledge <u>is</u> key to the decision. Obviously the key pre-decision is selecting the best expert! A variation on this is where the expert only brings a recommendation – it is still up to the team to accept it or reject it (using the other decision making styles).

6. *Authority Rule Without Discussion*
This is where there is usually no room for discussion, as with predetermined decisions handed down from higher authority. Trust is often killed with this method.

7. Authority Rule With Discussion

This method is also known as Participative Decision Making. Under this method, those in the decision making role make it clear from the onset that the task of decision making is theirs. Then, they join in a lively discussion of the issues. Their opinions count just like other team members. When they have heard enough to make an educated decision, they cut off the discussion, make the decision, and then get back to all team members to let them know how their inputs affected their decision.

Self-Reflection on your Team Decision-Making

- To what degree does your team use recognised decision-making techniques appropriate to different situations - *Largely, Partially or Not at all*?
- What is the best thing about your Team Decision-Making and how could this be really developed and extended?
- What is the **one thing** about your Team Decision-Making that is missing or could be done differently?

C4: Information Sharing

A few years back whilst I was writing the Bioteams book [A9], I conducted some applied research based on interviews to establish the beliefs and values of HPTs and how these contrasted with other less successful teams.

I identified 7 key team beliefs [A5, Appendix 3] which seemed to distinguish HPTs from lesser performing teams, one of which was **Total Transparency** which was defined as:

"HPT team members expect to be kept appraised in an honest and timely manner of any important issues in the project even if it does not directly affect them. This is part of the dynamic of every member believing they are a team leader and able to contribute beyond their specific functional team member briefs. They also believe they are free to pass opinions about situations they are not directly responsible for and these opinions should be respected and listened to."

In practical terms, therefore, teams need to decide when and how they will share information.

In terms of the "how," they have to consider the pros and cons of verbal information sharing during meetings versus sharing by email outside of meetings. Verbal sharing in meetings is very effective, but can consume valuable meeting time. Sharing by email is very efficient but some people may not read the emails. In practice, teams often come up with a hybrid solution where routine information is shared by email and other less predictable or sensitive information is shared verbally in meetings.

In practice, also there will always be some element of certain information which is on a "need to know" basis. However, my own experience in teams, networks and collaborative supply chains is that the more information you can share the better, and that people will generally respect information which is shared on the understanding that is to be treated as confidential or sensitive.

Self-Reflection on your Team Information-Sharing

- To what degree does your team effectively share accountabilities, priorities, updates and information - *Largely, Partially or Not at all?*
- What is the <u>best thing</u> about your Team Information-Sharing and how could this be really developed and extended?
- What is the **one thing** about your Team Information-Sharing that is missing or could be done differently?

4.4 Team Support & Systems

The final aspect of the HPTs Process Framework is having the right relationships and supporting processes and systems in place between team members to foster experience sharing, learning and prevention of potential problems BEFORE they occur.

S1: Personal Development

Recent research by *Deloitte* into organizational value suggests that all else being equal, a high performing organization is up to 70% more valuable than a low performing organization. This indicates the scope for personal development within a team; if they can become high performing they can be worth up to 70% more to their parent organization!

To achieve this, the leaders of such a team need to ensure that there are formal mechanisms in the team to create space for reflection and to allow best practice and learning from others mistakes to be routinely shared between the team members.

For example, within the world of software teams, there is a concept known as *Egoless Programming,* where developers are encouraged to read and review each other's code.

This is founded on the psychological concept of "cognitive dissonance" where we tend to see what we want to see rather than a more objective vision. This manifests itself when I read my own software code by only allowing me to see what I want to see and missing obvious errors in logic.

The results of such third party reviews of code (and other technical documents) is quite staggering. Simply put, team member code reviews are the most effective defect identification technique available to software developers by an order of magnitude!

HPTs invest in systematic recurrent processes to enable team members to develop new skills and to help and learn from each other.

<u>Self-Reflection on your Team Member Personal Development</u>

- To what degree does your team ensure personal development for all team members - *Largely, Partially or Not at all?*
- What is the <u>best thing</u> about your Team Member Personal Development and how could this be really developed and extended?
- What is the **one thing** about your Team Member Personal Development that is missing or could be done differently?

S2: Coaching Relationships

In his exceptional book, *Coaching – Evoking Excellence in Others*, James Flaherty suggests that 'interventions in competence to improve the actions of others' should only be called 'coaching' if they adhere to the following 5 operating principles:

1.   *Relationship*
Based on a relationship of mutual respect, mutual trust and freedom of expression.
2.   *Pragmatism*
Based not on abstract theory but on the principle 'what true is what works'.
3.   *Two Tracks*
An engaged learning experience for both the client and the coach.
4.   *Always/Already*
Respectful that those being coached are not empty vessels and bring with them their own unique life experiences and ways of dealing with things.
5.   *Techniques don't work*
Not reliant on selecting the right coaching 'techniques' as a substitute for absence of any of the other 4 operating principles.

There are many different approaches you can use for coaching. The most important thing is that you use something that feels comfortable to you personally. Otherwise you run the risk of failing one of Flaherty's 5 coaching operating principles such as being seen as too technique-based.

At the very simplest level you might use 'Instant Payoff Coaching' described in *The Tao of Coaching*, by Max Landsberg, which can be summarised in 4 simple steps

A Systematic Guide to
High Performing Teams (HPTs)

1.   Define the Problem
2.   Define the Ideal Outcome
3.   Identify the Blocks (in the 'coachee' and elsewhere)
4.   Brainstorm Solutions

This very simple coaching process also serves to illustrate two distinct development schools which coaches need to appreciate. By focusing on the problem and the blocks we are employing what is known as a 'problem-based coaching' approach to personal development.

The alternative is a 'strengths-based' approach to coaching where an instant payoff coaching process might look more like this:

1.   Agree some ambitions in an area
2.   Take stock of where the coachee has started and how far they have progressed
3.   Identify the strengths and skills which enabled this t
4.   Brainstorm about how the coachee could exploit these strengths to go even further

A good example of a strengths-based coaching approach is described in the popular 2004 book *Now, Discover Your Strengths* by Marcus Buckingham.

Problem-based and Strengths-based approaches both have their merits and supporters. It is, of course, entirely possible for a coach to use a 'hybrid approach' where they can draw from either approach depending on specific situations over the course of an on-going coaching relationship.

Mentoring: A Guide to the Basics by Gordon Shea (1992) suggests that 'A good mentor or coach will do one of these things for you and if you are lucky a great one might do all three':

- Provide an "aha" experience
- Offer a saying or quote that helps you spot a behaviour to seek or avoid
- Help uncover an aspect or talent which until then had laid dormant.

Research by my colleague Jay Cross and published in his excellent book *Informal Learning* suggests that up to 95% of the skills people need to do their day to day jobs are not learned "formally" but "Informally".

The 3 main techniques which constitute informal learning are:
1. Learning from your mistakes
2. Self-directed research/reading
3. Mentoring and coaching

So mentoring and coaching is not only a vital component of informal learning in itself, it also underpins the other 2 techniques by helping people get a good perspective on their mistakes and pointing them at highly targeted reading materials.

A true HPT will have rich coaching and mentoring relationships between the more experienced and less experienced team members. The more experienced will be sensitive and humble in their coaching styles, and the less experienced colleagues will be grateful and respectful of the time and commitment shown by their more experienced colleagues in offering coaching to them.

Self-Reflection on your Team Coaching

- To what degree are your team leader(s) in on-going coaching conversations with other team members - *Largely, Partially or Not at all*?
- What is the <u>best thing</u> about your Team Coaching and how could this be really developed and extended?
- What is the **one thing** about your Team Coaching that is missing or could be done differently?

S3: Peer Support System

Earlier, I mentioned my applied research project to establish the beliefs and values of HPTs [A5, Appendix 3] and how these contrasted with other teams.

I identified 7 key beliefs which seemed to distinguish HPTs from lesser performing teams, one of which was **Give and Take** defined as:

Give and Take

"HPT team members believe that if they need help they can ask for it and it will be freely offered. They believe that asking for help, in moderation, actually increases their standing within the team rather than diminishing it. They also believe something is badly wrong if somebody is struggling along and not asking for help or is asking for help but being ignored by the team".

- It is a very weak team if all help must flow between the leaders and the team members needing assistance.

- It is nearly as bad if all requests for and offers of help have to be channelled through the leaders.

- It's equally bad if help only flows from certain *stronger* members of the team to other *weaker* ones.

- It is just as bad if some team members feel that other team members will be offended by their offers of help because, for example, those offering help are more junior.

Whilst it is true that the most experienced team members should be able to help the less experienced team members more than the other way around, this is not the whole story. For example, junior team members may be able to help more experienced team members see things differently through a fresh set of eyes.

The optimum scenario is when requests for and offers of help flow freely between team members on a peer to peer basis across experience levels without the team leaders even noticing.

This is true a characteristic of an HPT.

Self-Reflection on your Team Peer Support System

- To what degree do team members directly support and help each through collaboration - *Largely, Partially or Not at all*?
- What is the best thing about your Team Peer Support and how could this be really developed and extended?
- What is the **one thing** about your Team Peer Support that is missing or could be done differently?

S4: Early Warning System

Bioteams Rule 2: Team Intelligence

Mobilize everyone to look for and manage team threats and opportunities.

In traditional teams, it's the leader's job to provide most of the "Team Intelligence," information on potential threats to, or opportunities for, the team. In a bioteam, it is every team member's responsibility to constantly look out for relevant team intelligence and to ensure it is instantly communicated to all other team members through a small but complete set of message protocols.

When I used to lead software teams, I discovered the amazing phenomenon of "crossing the line" in a team or project.

Before the line is crossed, each team member believes in the collective success of the team or project. Because of this, all the team members keep an eye out for each other and will flag up issues which they think might affect other team members even if they have no impact on themselves.

This is an effective team early warning system.

Frequently, however, projects and teams "cross the line", often due to unsupportive team leadership, and team members stop believing in collective success being likely.

Instead, they now believe the team or project is doomed to fail (though none may dare say this openly) and their focus changes from *aiming for the collective credit of success to avoiding the individual blame of failure.*

"This project is not going to work but nobody is going to be able to blame me."

Such a team no longer has a functioning team early warning system and every team member must spot and dodge their own "incomings" personally.

Teams without a functioning early warning system are unlikely to achieve high performance!

There is an excellent example of a team early warning system in Matthew Syed's excellent book 'Black Box'. Matthew describes how, after a particularly bad plane crash (United Airlines 173), where warnings by junior crew members were ignored by the captain, NASA introduced the, what was then, brand new discipline of Crew Resource Management.

As part of this system, to improve the assertiveness of junior members of crew, the mnemonic P.A.C.E was introduced:

- P – Probe
- A – Alert
- C – Challenge
- E - Emergency

Does your team have an Early Warning System and even if it does how do you know it is still switched on?

Self-Reflection on your Team Early Warning System

- To what degree do team members keep a lookout for any risks which might impact other team member's ability to deliver their results - *Largely, Partially or Not at all*?
- What is the <u>best thing</u> about your Team Early Warning System and how could this be really developed and extended?
- What is the **one thing** about your Team Early Warning System that is missing or could be done differently?

5. SUPPORTING TOOLS FOR CREATING HPTs

This section describes 3 useful tools to help you create HPTs:

- Team Process Health Check Spreadsheet
- High Performing Teams Simulation Game
- Team Leadership Simulation Game

Let's look at each in turn:

5.1 Team Process Health Check Spreadsheet

The image below is a screenshot from a Team Process Health Check Spreadsheet written in *Microsoft Excel*. It allows you to assess each of the 16 process elements on a scale of 0-3 ranging from totally absent to present and effective. The results are shown graphically as a bar chart (summary level) and a spider diagram (detailed level).

The spreadsheet also allows you to record your action priority (1-3) for each of the 16 process elements which it then compares automatically with the process maturity model described in section 3 to give you a good indication of whether your proposed sequence of process improvements makes sense in terms of relative process importance.

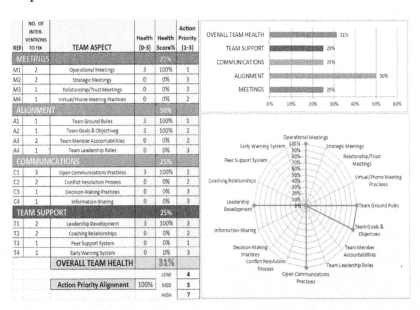

If you would like to obtain a free copy of the **Team Process Healthcheck Spreadsheet** please email me at www.dashboardsimulations.com

5.2 High Performing Teams Simulation Game

The CHAPTER Simulation is a unique resource, which allows prospective team leaders and managers to practice their skills *building* an HPT in a safe environment, is a computer based business simulation game designed around all the concepts discussed in this book.

The screenshot overleaf is from the main simulation decision making screen which presents players with the opportunity to try out all the change management and process development interventions discussed in this book with a newly formed team of 10 members.

As part of the simulation, the players analyse all the briefing material on the fictitious company. Briefing materials, in the forms of bios, are also provided for each team member along with a team organization chart and social network.

The briefing materials provide the necessary information to determine the required change management intervention per individual and also allow the players to conduct an initial team process heath check on the team as a whole.

The simulation itself is played in teams and uses the latest experiential and social learning techniques to amplify the learning. Simulations typically run for half a day with 3-4 teams each of 4-6 players.

For more on CHAPTER see www.dashboardsimulations.com.

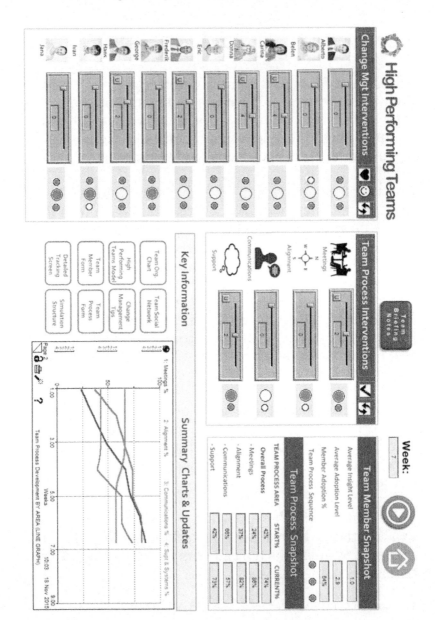

5.3 Team Leadership Simulation Game

The CREW Simulation is an online game which allows team leaders and prospective team leaders to experience some of the challenges in *leading* a High Performing Team.
CREW is complementary to CHAPTER (see 5.2). CHAPTER is about setting up and bedding down an HPT whereas CREW is about leading and managing such a team on an on-going basis.

The scenario in CREW is that you have 5 team colleagues in your team and you must manage their workload, personal, team and any project issues which occur in a 4-week period played in a half day simulation session.

The guidance offered throughout this guide is very relevant to the challenges offered by CREW and in particular Chapter 6, The 7 habits of great team leaders.

The main CREW screen is shown overleaf:

- The Top Left Quadrant shows how you are doing against your various KPIs as a Team Leader.
- The Bottom Left Quadrant shows the status of all the task your team is responsible for and allows you as team leader to intervene in any task as required.
- The Top Right Quadrant shows the 'health indicators' of your team members and allows you to select individual and team interventions.
- The Bottom Left Quadrant is where you allocate your colleagues and yourself to the various tasks with the objective of having them complete on schedule and to the customer's satisfaction.

For more on CREW see www.dashboardsimulations.com.

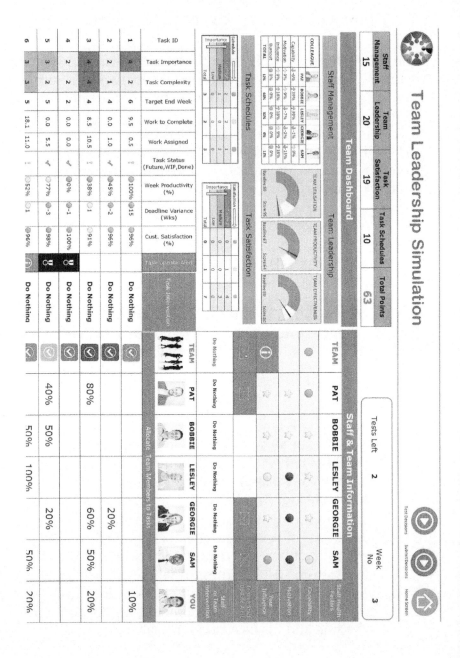

6. SEVEN HABITS OF GREAT TEAM LEADERS

So now you have started to make the necessary change management and process interventions required to establish a High Performing Team. Even though you are 'creating the conditions' for your team's success your organization will not yet have gained any significant value from all your hard work!

Your team will only generate value for your organization through what they achieve moving forward and this will depend how well they are led. You need to turn all this 'potential' you have built into 'profits'! You have 2 key leadership tasks to which you must now apply yourself on an on-going basis:

      A. Manage the Individuals
      B. Manage the Team

As a slight digression, we can compare this simplified 2-dimensional Team Leadership model with two other very important 3-dimensional models. The first is John Adair's *Action Centred Leadership* model which has as its 3 dimensions of **Team, Task and Individual**. The second is a model, credited by James Flaherty in his Coaching book as being inspired by the influential German philosopher Jurgen Habermas and offering its 3 dimensions of **I, We and It**.

These two models appear quite similar although the Habermas definition of 'We' encompasses 'Relationships with others' which is wider than Adair's 'Team'. The 2-dimensional Team Leadership model proposed here simplifies things by dropping the Task/IT dimension altogether. The rationale being that much of this work is the responsibility of the team member and not a leadership concern. However, I attempt to mitigate the effects of this simplification (at least on a relational level) by adding the Customer (relationship) into the 'Managing the Team' dimension.

MANAGE THE INDIVIDUALS

Through your initial change management work you should now have a much greater insight into your team members. You must continue to build this insight and of course your relationships which underpin everything.

It's useful to develop the leadership discipline of constantly being able to do a quick 'team temperature check' of the people you are responsible for from 3 different perspectives or lenses.

Habit 1: Manage the Person

- What kind of personality have they?
- In what ways are they different from you?
- What is important to them outside work?
- What is important to them in work?
- What challenges/pressures are they facing at home?
- What challenges/pressures are they facing at work?
- **Are they in an 'OK' place as people?**

Habit 2: Manage the Professional

- How good are their job specific skills (e.g. Web design or production engineering)?
- How strong are their interpersonal skills?
- How good is their leadership/potential?
- What are their strengths and weaknesses?
- How actively are they being developed through training and/or coaching?
- **Are they in an 'OK' place as professionals?**

Habit 3: Manage the Colleague

- How do they get on with the other team members?
- Who do they struggle with?
- Who do they work well with?
- What positives and negatives do they bring to team meetings?
- **Are they in an 'OK' place as team members?**

MANAGE THE TEAM

In simple terms there are 4 main aspects of managing the team:

Habit 4: Manage the Team's Workload

It is important to balance the demands coming into the team with the resources available to meet those demands. For each task you will have to decide who should do it primarily taking into account availability, capacity and capability. However, these are not the only points to consider.

You will also need to think about giving people the opportunity to learn by doing tasks which will stretch them – possibility with a more experienced team member acting as a coach. You also need to think about boredom where a task is no longer challenging to an individual. If you keep asking them to do it over and over again they will get bored and de-motivated and even leave.

If you are a 'hands-on' team leader you also need to think about what tasks you specifically pick up. This shows your team that you are not afraid to get your hands dirty. However, you must be careful not just to select the most interesting or best jobs. Also you must be careful not to over-schedule yourself. Over-scheduling can be a comfort blanket for a team leader who does not feel comfortable with engaging properly with and looking after their team members.

Habit 5: Manage the Team's Energy Levels

It is your job as team leader to look after the people on your team. If you push them too hard then they may become burned out. If you don't push them enough they may become demotivated. You should also be on the lookout for early warning signs of developing problems.

For example, if a colleague has become unusually sullen or irritable are they feeling the pressure and on their way to a period of stress leave which you could nip in the budget?

Alternatively, if a colleague is starting to take unexplained days off work they could be applying for other jobs because they are not happy in their work?

On the other hand, if they are not using up their leave or always seeking overtime then this could be pointing at other issues such as financial worries? When did you last review their salaries? What home pressures are they under? Have they a new baby in the family? Has their partner lost their job?

As a team leader you need to develop effective early people warning systems and be skilful in having conversations with colleagues where you suspect something might be 'off'.

Your job as team leader is to spot and eliminate any **'barriers or blockers'** which drain team energy levels.

Habit 6: Manage the Team's Customers

Your team exists to serve its customers. They can be external customers or internal customers or a combination. A good team leader will develop an awareness of the team's customers. Such a team leader will also be looking wherever possible to create direct customer relationships. This can be very helpful as long as it does not appear that you are under-cutting or not trusting your team colleagues.

This is also an important component of your early warning system as it can tell you if projects are going wrong. If you have the right relationships with your customers, they may also give you quiet 'heads-up' of people issues too.

Habit 7: Manage the Team's Practices

The fourth aspect of being a good team leader is to be constantly looking at the team's processes and practices to see how they could be improved. Don't be fooled into a false sense of security by the fact that you have just introduced new HPT practices. These processes and practices can fossilise just like any others. You need to keep checking are they still being used, are they producing value and what way could they be improved.

Over to you
You could now take this opportunity to conduct a quick
assessment of your own team leadership against these 7
habits represented graphically overleaf

Step#1 – Self Assessment
Against each of the 7 habits first estimate what percentage
of your <u>working time</u> you allocate to each on a typical
week. This is really an assessment of your *priorities* as a
team leader. Be interested in how much time you spend in
areas not covered by the 7 habits. What insights can you
take from this? Now score yourself against each of the
habits in terms of how *effective* you think you are using a
simple 4-point scale e.g.

1 = Less than effective
2 = Satisfactory
3 = Good
4 = Very effective

Step#2 - Peer Assessment
Now meet with a peer in a similar role as yourself and each
assess the other. Where does your colleague reach different
assessments about your effectiveness? What insights can
you take from this?

Step#3 – Team Assessment
This is the most useful step and the one which requires the
most courage in a leader! Ask your team members to do
their honest assessments of you on both time and
effectiveness. Make them anonymous and prepare a
summary showing your average, highest and lowest scores
for each habit? Present the results back to your team and
invite comment. What insights can you take from this?

7-HABITS TEAM LEADERSHIP ASSESSMENT MODEL

Copyright Ken Thompson 2015

If you would like to obtain a free copy of the supporting **Team Leadership Assessment Spreadsheet** please email me at
www.dashboardsimulations.com

7: THE TEAM DILEMMA

The Team dilemma is how we balance the tensions of being an effective, autonomous and motivating leader with being a supportive and loyal member of a senior team.

The Team dilemma is essentially a 'Me vs. We' conundrum. It encompasses all the tensions individuals face in leading teams at the same time as being members of other teams in which they are not the leader.

The 3 main areas of the Team dilemma are:

- Conflicting Styles
- Decisions and Decision-Making
- Coordination

Conflicting Styles

A wise person once said if you find the perfect team don't join it as you will spoil it. You can't be in an organization without being in a team and colleagues will annoy, exasperate and frustrate you. Whether we like it or not we have exactly the same effect on our colleagues.

What are the most common areas for friction around colleagues' personalities, behaviours and styles? One way to look at this is through personality tests. There are many different types of test each of which use a different lens to look at people. One of the most popular is the *Myers Briggs Type Indicator* (MBTI) [1] which categorizes individuals across 4 preferences:

1. Our favourite World
Are we Extraverts (E) or Introverts (I)?

Do we prefer the outer world or our own inner world?

2. How we handle Information
Are we sensing (S) or are we Intuitive (N)?

'Sensors' prefer to focus only on the raw information whereas 'Intuitives' prefer to interpret information and add their own meaning?

3. How we make Decisions
Are we Thinking (T) or Feeling (F)?

'Thinkers' prefer to look at logic and consistency whereas 'Feelers' prefer to look more at the people and any special circumstances?

4. How to we like to Resolve things
Are we Judging (J) or Perceiving (P)?

'Judgers' prefer to get things decided whereas 'Perceivers' prefer to stay open and receptive to new information and options?

In MBTI an individual is classified according to the 4 preferences which creates 16 different possibilities. For example, an 'ENTJ' prefers the outer world, likes the big picture, is very logical about decisions and likes to get things resolved quickly.

On the other hand, an 'ISFP' is the polar opposite of an ENTJ preferring their inner world and the details of a situation. They also prefer to be more intuitive about decisions and don't need to decide so quickly. It is easy to see the tensions which an ENTJ might have working closely in a team with an ISFP.

Just to be clear I am NOT putting forward MBTI as a recommended approach in your organization. Like all tests MBTI has a number of short-comings which are well documented [2]. However, I AM suggesting it can provide a useful way to see obvious areas of potential conflict between team members.

So to be more effective in dealing with team members it is helpful if we can develop an awareness of each other's styles and preferences. We don't have to do personality tests – we can simply talk with each other about would what we prefer in key areas such as:

- Listening vs. Talking
- Disclosing vs. Not Disclosing 'personal things'
- Information – do we prefer more or less?
- Thinking Time – do we prefer like to get information in advance of discussing?

Decisions and decision-making

Decisions and decision-making are two areas in themselves that can cause a huge amount of conflict between individuals in teams.

In terms of the *actual decisions* made it won't be long before we find ourselves holding the opposite position from some of our team members on a particular decision. If we feel strongly about it, we can try and win our colleagues around but this won't always succeed. Even if we do succeed in winning them round we may have alienated or bullied them in the process. So a frequent dilemma is whether any particular team decision is worth taking an individual stand over?

The next dilemma is where we have not been able to win our colleagues around (or decided not to try!) We can find ourselves in a team who have made a decision we don't agree with. This brings us to 'collective responsibility' or 'cabinet responsibility' as it is referred to in government.

We have to decide can we live with and actively support a decision which we don't agree with. Hopefully we can do this in most cases but if we can't we need to decide the best way to handle it. Ways NOT to handle it include keeping trying to re-run the team arguments to change the decision back or telling colleagues outside the team that the team has made a big mistake but you have to go along with it!

The second area for conflict is HOW the decisions are actually reached in the first place. In the excellent book, "Why Teams Don't Work" [3], the authors identify 7 key decision making styles for teams. If a team is planning to make a major decision, it should, wherever possible, discuss and agree on how the decision will be reached (e.g. using one of these 7 styles) before the actual decision-making discussions start.

At the meeting, the team leader should introduce the decision which needs to be made and then propose the decision making style which is then discussed and agreed:
1. Consensus
2. Majority Rule
3. Minority Rule
4. Averaging
5. Expert
6. Authority Rule without Discussion
7. Authority Rule with Discussion

Earlier in this book, (chapter 3) I discuss decision-making and the related topic of effective team meetings in more detail.

Coordination

The third dilemma for an individual in a team is how they handle the need to receive and give help and feedback. We all know people who function at various extremes. There are the 'lone rangers' who can delegate nothing or ever ask for help. There are the 'micro-managers' who try to do their colleagues jobs as well as their own. There are also the 'Teflons' which nothing ever sticks to. 'Teflons' somehow seem to manage to avoid picking up any direct commitments or responsibilities whatever themselves.

What is really going on with these behavioural stereotypes?

If you look below the surface you will see that there are a couple of important values conversations which need to be had around Trust, Respect and Commitment:

- Will I trust you with my reputation?
- Will I respect your reputation?
- Am I willing to make commitments to you?
- Will I trust the commitments you make to me?

If you see these stereotypes of bad co-ordination in your team it is often a warning that you need to revisit your team values (refer to the chapter on the Planning Dilemma) and/or your commitment management processes (refer to the chapter on the Agility Dilemma).

SELF-REFLECTION EXERCISE

1. *How/where does the 'Team Dilemma' manifest itself most strongly in your organization or team?*

2. *Can you identify some recent examples where difficult choices had to be made around Team?*

3. *Can you select one of these examples and use the Creative Dilemma Resolution process to brainstorm an alternative response?*

FURTHER READING on Team

1. The Myers Briggs Foundation, http://www.myersbriggs.org/my-mbti-personality-type/mbti-basics/
2. The Myth of Personality Types: Exposing Pop Psychology's Biggest Scam, Chance Ableson, Re Wired Books, 2016
3. *Why Teams Don't Work*: Robbins, Harvey, and Michael Finley, January 2000

=====

The Team Dilemma is one of ten core business and leadership dilemmas explored in my book 'The Systematic Guide to Business Acumen and Leadership using Dilemmas'.

=====

8: INSTANT TEAM – HPTs IN A HURRY!

Can you create a High-Performing Team in a day or afternoon or even over lunch? Of course not!

However, if you are put in the position where you, as a leader, have to get the very best out of a group of colleagues in very short timescales what can you do?

Here is my 4-step approach to 'Instant Team'.

STEP1: Create Team 'Game Plan'

Below is my 7-point checklist which teams can use to produce a Team Game Plan (1-2 pages maximum):

1.   **R**oles
How will we divide up the team responsibilities?
2.   **A**greements (Ground Rules)
How will we deal with each other as colleagues and team members?
3.   **P**rocesses/Practices
What are the 2-3 most important team processes/practices will we put in place and follow?
4.   **P**riorities
How will we decide what is most important, particularly in dilemmas or under pressure? [2]
5.   **O**rganizational Values
What values are the most important to us as a team?
6.   **R**esults
What specific results must we achieve as our minimum team performance level?
7.   **T**argets
What is our 'stretch' target, our ambition to exceed our minimum performance level?

The first letter of each element spells 'R.A.P.P.O.R.T.' which is a useful mnemonic for a Team Game Plan. This is apt as 'Rapport' can be defined as *'A close and harmonious relationship in which the groups concerned understand each other's feelings or ideas and communicate well'* according to THE OXFORD DICTIONARY.

STEP 2: Test the Team

Do some short team-based activity as a Team and try to follow your Team Game Plan. You need to set aside at least 1 hour but 3 hours is better. If you have 3 hours, you can play a team-based business simulation or even some off-site activity. If you only have 1 hour you can still have a team problem-solving brainstorming meeting on a practical topic with which everyone is already familiar.

STEP 3: Reflect and Improve

At the end of this team activity, team members should take at least 30 minutes to discuss and reflect on a small number of key questions typically:

- How well are we working as a team – what could we improve?
- What would we do differently if we did the activity again?
- How closely are we following our team game plan – does this need to be revised?

If you have 2-3 hours, then you can conduct this review more than once as this allows the team to see visible improvements quickly. Another very useful device is to have the teams self-assess against the *'7 mistakes teams make under pressure'* (see overleaf).

A Systematic Guide to
High Performing Teams (HPTs)

The '7 mistakes' have been gathered over ten years and represent the most common mistakes teams make participating in team-based business simulation games.

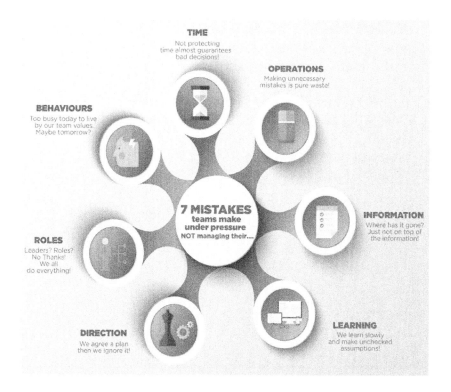

STEP 4: Execute and Review

Now you need to direct the team to the job in hand with the specific extra directive of 'Follow your Game Plan!' In addition, you must build in a regular (e.g. weekly) review cycle where you repeat the self-reflection/improvement from Step 4 using, of course, all the other guidance and tools offered in the rest of the book!

The evolution of team working

If you observe newly formed and existing teams playing business simulations and other intensive challenges, you can gain some important insights into how team-working actually 'evolves'. This knowledge can help you accelerate the evolution of effective team working and collaboration in your own organizational teams.

On the road to Effective Team Collaboration there seems to be two intermediate phases of 'naïve collaboration' which teams often seem to go through - *Hyper-Communication* and *Over-Delegation.*

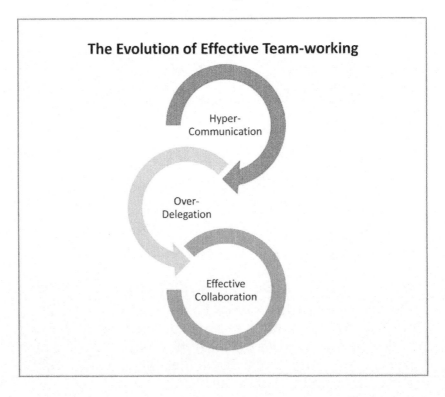

The Evolution of Effective Team-working

Hyper-Communication

Over-Delegation

Effective Collaboration

A Systematic Guide to
High Performing Teams (HPTs)

PHASE 1: Hyper-Communication

In this phase almost every team member is involved in almost every team conversation. It is very democratic and feels really good but the problem is that it just takes forever. A team operating like this will not hit its deadlines.

An organisational team meeting which conducts its operational meetings like this will not get through its agenda. In my experience teams usually start here on their journey towards effective collaboration. Teams in this phase genuinely believe that they are collaborating well UNTIL they suddenly discover that working like this is just not practical as it simply takes too long!

When teams have tried 'Hyper-Communication' they often *over-correct* and move to the next phase of naive collaboration: 'Over-Delegation'.

PHASE 2: Over-Delegation

In this phase the team quickly agree that they need to work faster and more efficiently. To achieve this, they wisely decide that they need some roles and division of labour but they 'over-delegate'. By this I mean they give out jobs to the different members and sub-teams but do not support this with sufficient communications to ensure they all stay on the same page.

Like the first phase, Hyper-Communication, teams think they have fixed their collaboration and they feel they are being very efficient UNTIL they discover, typically near the end of the round, that they are no longer all on the same page and that the team members have been working to different assumptions and priorities which invalidates much of their good work.

PHASE 3: Effective Collaboration

Once teams have experienced both of these naïve forms of collaboration (Hyper-Communication and Over-Delegation) they are well placed to find a middle ground with represents Effective Collaboration.

As with Over-Delegation they allocate roles but this time they also ensure that this is supported by on-going communications particularly around task objectives and early review of provisional findings/decisions before they become finalised.

Accelerated Team Development

From these insights it is clear that many teams find it very difficult to move directly into Effective Collaboration without first experiencing **and learning** from both Hyper-Communication and Over-Delegation.

I can't prove it but feel strongly that it may also be the case that many organisational teams simply *flip-flop* between the two naïve collaboration phases of Hyper-Communication and Over-Delegation without ever making the break-through into Effective Collaboration ... perhaps all the time believing, they are already doing it!

A Systematic Guide to
High Performing Teams (HPTs)

Therefore, to fast track effective team-working you need 3 simple ingredients:

1. **Mechanisms such as competitive business simulation games** or other short team challenges.

2. **Briefing for the teams on the challenges with specific deadlines and goals** but without any instruction about how they are to behave other than that they are a team.

3. **Facilitated team self-analysis sessions at the end of each round** or chunk of work to let teams review what kind of collaboration they are employing and how they might improve it.

If you carefully and skilfully work with these 3 ingredients, you can help teams in your organization develop effective team-working and collaboration skills in a much faster timescale than might be possible using other methods.

9: TEAM PRESSURE COOKER EXERCISE

Sometimes teams can become quite blind towards some very obvious improvements to their performance. There may be *huge elephants in the team room* which have somehow become camouflaged.

Here is a short team exercise to quickly highlight big improvement opportunities by putting the team into an imaginary pressure cooker.

Step 1: Select a Project

Invite the team to select a project they are in the middle of or have just recently completed.

Step 2: X-Ray Project

Summarise the selected project according to 4 key dimensions:

- The Timeline (Stressor 1)
- The Team (Stressor 2)
- The Main Team Project Outcome (Stressor 3)
- The Importance of the Team Project Outcome to the Organization (Stressor 4)

If the team cannot do this quickly it is a sure sign that something is wrong - you would not have much confidence in a sports team where the players in the locker room could not agree on the goal before a big match!

Step 3: Stress the Project

Now stress the team in each of the 4 dimensions.

This is best done as a team exercise with the selected action decided by discussion/vote but it can also be used privately by the team leader(s) as an on-going sanity check:

Stressor 1 - Time

What is the one thing you would have to do to succeed if .... your delivery deadline is brought forward significantly - e.g. 6 months becomes 3 months? Restrict it to one proposed action only.

Stressor 2 - Resources

What is the one thing you would have to do to succeed if .... your resources are significantly cut – e.g. assume each team member is now only available half of the time they were before? Restrict it to one proposed action only.

Stressor 3 - Scope

What is the one thing you would have to do to succeed if .... you now have to deliver twice as much as originally planned? Restrict it to one proposed action only.

Stressor 4 - Consequences

What is the one thing you would have to do to succeed if .... failure to meet the new deadline, with the new resources and new scope was absolutely business critical. For example, the organization closes and the team members all lose their jobs? Restrict it to one proposed action only.

Turning the pressure up

There are two ways you can do this – the gentle way is that each stressor is applied independently.

The much more interesting way is if the effect of each stressor is *cumulative* – in other words you first encounter the time pressure then you also encounter the resources pressure then you also encounter the scope pressure then on top of all this you encounter the consequences pressure!

Step 4: Implement the Findings

Now you need to decide which Stressor Actions to implement NOW in the team. Review the 4 proposed actions and for each one ask the simple question:

'Is there a compelling reason why we should not do this NOW for the current team project/projects/situation?'

Outcomes and benefits from the Pressure Cooker Exercise

In my experience applying the 4 stressors will result in actions such as:

- Stressor 1 - Meet with the team's customer to understand what is absolutely critical to them and negotiate anything else out of scope.

- <u>Stressor 2</u> - Have a short daily structured team meeting by phone - totally focussed.

- <u>Stressor 3</u> - Have a no 'BS' conversation with every team member to ensure they are clear and committed to what needs done and that all barriers to success they can identify are removed.

- <u>Stressor 4</u> - Secure additional help (resources, skills, relationships, money...) outside the immediate project team - don't take no for an answer!

Usually these actions should have been implemented anyway.

The '4 Team Stressors' only serve to bring into sharp focus what the <u>team already knew needed done but did not know they knew!</u>

10: SUCCESSFULLY RUNNING LARGE MEETINGS

Some of my work as a consultant involves facilitating large meetings or workshops where groups, often from different departments or even different organizations, must collaborate to resolve difficult issues or develop future plans for working together.

I have developed 7 rules which I now share with participants in advance and have them 'sign-up' to before we start the meetings on the promise, from me, that the results will be well worth the initial discomfort of running these meetings in a very different way than they are used to!

EGOLESS MEETINGS

I call this concept 'Egoless Meetings' and it has 2 key components - 'Trustful Collaboration' and 'Disciplined Discussion'.

The first 4 rules are about how people should behave in terms of being effective collaborators with people with diverse interests some of whom they may be meeting for the very first time ('Trustful Collaboration').

The remaining 3 rules concern how discussions can be conducted when there are many participants wanting to speak but yet time is constrained ('Disciplined Discussions').

A Systematic Guide to
High Performing Teams (HPTs)

THE 4 RULES OF TRUSTFUL COLLABORATION

RULE 1: Don't make people earn your trust

What percentage of the general population do you believe to be untrustworthy? Is it >5%, > 10%, >15%, > 20%?

In the excellent book The Sociopath Next Door [1] Harvard Medical School psychiatrist *Martha Stout* reveals that as many as **4%** of the population are 'conscienceless sociopaths' who have no empathy or affectionate feelings for humans or animals. A sociopath is defined as someone who displays at least three of seven distinguishing characteristics, such as deceitfulness, impulsivity and a lack of remorse. Such people often have a superficial charm, which they exercise ruthlessly in order to get what they want

Now the other side of that coin is this also means that 96% of people <u>are</u> trustworthy – i.e. 24 out of 25 people you meet. So it is not actually a big risk to start from a position of trust with other people. You can always 'revoke' your trust later if you need to. From a collaboration point of view this is much more productive than making the people you work with earn your trust first.

RULE 2: Don't criticise other's proposals - make a counter-proposal

When somebody makes a proposal you need to resist the natural urge to comment on or critique it as this will usually lead only to debate not action. It is much better to build on it or if you don't like it then make a counter-proposal or ask the person a clarifying question to draw out more details (but not a threatening or aggressive question.)

The theoretical background for this is that certain *speech acts* lead to action (Offers and Requests) and other speech actions lead to analysis (Opinions and Comments). Speech Acts are part of a popular change management discipline known as Commitment Based Management [2] which is used to improve the way people manage their promises in organisations.

RULE 3 - Focus on other's needs first - then they will focus on yours

Steven Covey, in his book The Seven Habits of Highly Effective People [3], says "seek first to understand before being understood". Collaboration works best when everybody focuses on the other participants' needs first. Paradoxically if everyone comes to the meeting fixated on their own needs then usually no one's needs get met.

So at the start of the process you should focus on the needs of the other participants and at the end of the process check whether your needs have been met. You will probably be pleasantly surprised. *I have a great story linking this point with difference between Heaven and Hell but you will have to be in the room with me to hear it live!*

RULE 4 - If in doubt reveal rather than conceal

I once facilitated a group of biotech scientists who were very reluctant to describe their work area in any detail to the other scientists because of concerns over IP

(Intellectual Property). It was like a Monty Python sketch. Guess what - nobody was able to collaborate! Sadly 100% of a very small pie is usually much less tasty than 25% of a very large pie.

Most of what we have in our heads is not in the "company secrets" category and can be freely shared with little risk. Don't make the other parties play *Sherlock Holmes* to work out what you want or need from the collaboration - put it straight out there - it saves so much time and energy!

THE 3 RULES OF DISCIPLINED DISCUSSION

RULE 5: It only needs said once - eliminate "ego-speak"

In traditional meetings there is an unspoken rule – everybody gets to speak. People come to meetings with an "expectation of airtime". This is often related to their grade or their perception of their role in the meeting. This means that everybody gets to speak even when they have nothing to say or are merely repeating what others have already said. This wastes time and saps the energy of the other participants. Political correctness means we feel we are being rude if we don't allow everyone to have their say. But this ultimately just wastes everyone's' time and many will vote with their feet by not returning to the next meeting.

This can be a tricky one to deal with as a meeting leader or facilitator. You can ignore it, you can placate it or even worse you can flip between trying to ignore and trying to placate it. I suggest a third approach to ego in meetings - eliminate it through process and practice. Take the ego out of the meeting by introducing mechanisms to discourage repetition and reward brevity and silence. You can easily do this is a fun way where nobody gets offended but with the desired effect.

RULE 6: If all else fails ... then discuss it

Many people come to meetings in a kind of "standby mode" or in a mood where the meeting is a break from "normal work". This can drive the meeting into a general discussion/ conversation mode in the name of "understanding each other better". These conversations are often "speak much - listen little" and usually only succeed in diverging and hardening the group member positions rather than converging them. The unfortunate scribe or facilitator then writes the meeting up but the notes are of little value and probably never referenced again.

When you feel a big unplanned discussion starting up you need to 'time out' the group and have the meeting quickly consider these 7 questions:

1. What is the objective and is it crystal clear?
2. Are people in the right frame of mind?
3. Are people really focused on the same topic?
4. What is the decision or action we must take and are we certain we can't make that decision without discussion?
5. Is this the first time we have discussed this matter?
6. If this discussion was all the meeting did would it be worth it?
7. Is this the minimum (not the maximum) set of people to have the discussion?

If you can't answer "Yes" to all 7 of these then don't have a discussion - address the issue in another way (See Rule 7).

RULE 7: Include non-whole-group work in all your meetings

There is another unspoken rule about meetings – 'When you meet as a team you must work as a team'. This is a great waster of meeting time - teams don't need to do everything as a team, even if they are all in the one room. They need to do individual work as a team as well. I call this kind of team work "solo" work where all the people in the room are doing a different thing at the same time rather than doing the same thing at the same time. In any creative or production process solo work is generally the best way to get the heavy lifting done - not group work!

When you convene a meeting you create the possibility of a number of "brains". The most obvious one is the collective brain of the whole group. But you also still have the individual brains of its members (solo work). In addition, there are other "brains" available to you - the brains of people when they pair up or work in groups of three - I call this pair work and triangle work. You can also create bigger group brains such as groups of 4 or splitting the group in two. The key point is that you should pick the most appropriate group brain for the task at hand and this is often not the whole group brain!

So, for example, instead of one person writing something and the whole team reviewing it how about each team member writes a paragraph, reviews it with a partner to see how it if it is "good enough" to be included in a collective first draft to be circulated after the meeting to the whole team.

Another example is 'ideas generation'. In the old model we do this as a group - in this new model we might generate our ideas totally individually by ourselves and present them to the group as seeds to a high-energy group innovation session. This resonates with Edward De Bono's thinking [4] on effective brain-storming and research which shows that the best ideas in brainstorms generally come near the end once all the obvious ideas have been exhausted and are often clever variants of earlier ideas.

Introducing Egoless Meetings into your organization

So what keep people running their meetings the old way if they are so bad? One answer might be the usual stuff - politeness, political correctness, laziness, fear, organizational inertia and groupthink. However, I prefer the answer that it is mostly ignorance and it is your job as a leader or facilitator is to show people that there actually is a viable and enjoyable alternative!

Now I am not saying that Egoless Meetings fully applies in all cases. For example, in meetings which are specifically about conflict resolution and trust-building, rather than action, then there clearly is a need for full and frank discussions and if you are constraining them this needs to be done with sensitivity. More importantly, however, in such meetings you need to allow enough time. If you find yourself facilitating conflict resolution under serious time pressure, then you only have yourself to blame for not designing the process correctly. However, in my experience, most meetings are about action and here the 7 rules of egoless meetings can really help.

If, however, most of your meetings are about conflict resolution and trust-building then you are really working in a truly awful place and good meeting practices are the very least of your worries!

References

1. The Sociopath Next Door, *Martha Stout,* Harmony, 2006
2. Commitment-based Management, http://www.managementexchange.com/hack/commitment-based-management-20-making-and-keeping-commitments
3. The 7 Habits of Highly Effective People: Powerful Lessons in Personal Change, *Stephen Covey,* Simon & Schuster, 1999
4. Serious Creativity: Using the Power of Lateral Thinking to Create New Ideas, *Edward De Bono*, 1995

11: INTER-TEAM RELATIONS

Do you ever wonder why is there so much politics between the teams in your organisation or why the departments in your enterprise always seem to be working to different agendas?

You might conclude it's all about the ambitions of the group leaders or the fact that the groups have to compete for scarce organizational resources? These were the dominant theories before the ground-breaking research of *Henri Tajfel*, a Polish Jew and social psychologist, who spent his life exploring the roots of prejudice, discrimination and persecution.

Tajfel discovered through a series of famous experiments (the 'minimal group' paradigm) that even groups which are totally constructed at random display automatic prejudices towards their own groups. Through research with school children in the UK in the 1970's, Tajfel discovered that the very act of categorising a person into a group (their 'in-group') causes them to favour that group over other groups (their 'out-groups').

Tajfel's proposes that we gain our self-esteem as humans by showing favour to our in-group and showing enmity and hostility towards any rival out-group. His research proves conclusively that destructive rivalry between organisational teams exists independently of the ambitions of the leaders and the competition for resources!

So if this conflict exists even in the "perfect organisation" then how much worse will it be in the typical organisation when we add in those two other factors – leadership ambition and competition for scarce resources?

A Systematic Guide to
High Performing Teams (HPTs)

So what does Tajfel's research mean for team leaders and leaders who are trying to create high performing teams in their organizations?

First, we need to accept this is the way things are whether we like it or not!

Secondly, we need to be committed to taking proactive and planed actions to diffuse and counter the natural inter-team rivalries. Tajfel suggests that strong on-going dialogue between the members and leaders of the different teams is required.

Also as team leaders, we can choose to model positive attitudes towards the out-teams in our organisation by speaking well about them. Also we can intervene in our in-teams when our colleagues start to scapegoat another team.

No person or team can succeed solely through its own resources and capabilities. At some critical point we will need help or a short-order favour! A good team leader does not just nurture good 'in-team' relations but also does whatever is required to develop good 'inter-team' relations with their organisational out-teams.

Such leaders recognise that that good inter-team relations are sadly not the default state in their organizations and will not improve without real effort and investment on their part.

Inter-team Relations: End Notes and Further reading

1.   For more on Social Identity Theory and the Minimal Group Paradigm you can listen to this excellent 30-minute BBC podcast:
http://www.bbc.co.uk/programmes/b00yw6km

2.   There is also a famous social simulation based on the 'Schelling Segregation Model' which shows what happens when you have two prejudiced groups living in the same place such as a city or a country. The shared living space in the simulation is modelled as a simple chessboard. Each house owner has a preference for living next to their own kind (race, tribe, religion, class, sexual preference etc). If this preference is met, then they stay where they are otherwise they move house which leads to self-organisation of the chessboard. *The simulation shows that even a mild preference for living next door to your 'own kind' soon produces a totally segregated society.* This is what I call a 'Eureka Simulation' as it can give players a blinding flash of insight, in this case, that even a very slight level of social intolerance can bring devastating consequences in the medium-long term.
http://nifty.stanford.edu/2014/mccown-schelling-model-segregation/

12. FURTHER READING

12.1 Ken Thompson's HPT Books, Videos & Articles

A1: TEDxBelfast - Ken Thompson - The 7 Habits of High Performing Teams
https://www.youtube.com/watch?v=KNNWLj-3wx0

A2: Ken Thompson - The Networked Enterprise – Presentation to NASA Langley Research Center https://vimeo.com/11269948

A3: The Bioteaming Manifesto
http://changethis.com/manifesto/show/19.BioteamingManifesto

A4: The secret DNA of high-performing teams
http://www.bioteams.com/2005/08/04/the_secret_dna.html

A5: Bioteams and the beliefs of high performing teams
http://www.bioteams.com/2011/11/24/bioteams_and_the.html

A6: TEN Great Bioteams Exercises for High-Performing Teams
http://www.bioteams.com/2010/11/02/ten_great_bioteams.html

A7: High performance leadership/decisions: business game research findings
http://www.bioteams.com/2013/05/25/high_performance_leadership_decisions.html

A8: A Collaboration Maturity Model
http://www.bioteams.com/2005/11/24/a_collaboration_maturity.html

A9: Bioteams: High Performance Teams Based on Nature's Most Successful Designs, Ken Thompson, Meghan-Kiffer Press, November 2008
https://www.amazon.com/Bioteams-Performance-Natures-Successful-Designs-ebook/dp/B00DFR11K8

A10: The Networked Enterprise: Competing for the Future Through Virtual Enterprise Networks, Ken Thompson, Meghan-Kiffer Press, June 2008
http://www.amazon.com/Networked-Enterprise-Competing-Through-Networks/dp/0929652452

12.2 Select Reading List on High Performing Teams

B1: *The Coming Shape of Organization*, Butterworth-Heinemann, Belbin, Meredith, May 1998.

B2: *Hot Groups – Seeding them, feeding them and using them to ignite your organization*, Lipman-Blumen, Jean, and Harold Leavitt, Oxford University Press, 1999.

B3: *Organizing Genius – The Secrets of Creative Collaboration*, Nicholas Brealey, 1997.

B4: *The Mythical Man Month*, Brooks, Fred, Addison-Wesley, 1995.

B5: *Teamwork in animals, robots and humans*, Anderson, Carl, and Nigel Franks, Advances in the Study of Behaviour, pp. 1-27, 1989.

B6: *Why Teams Don't Work*: Robbins, Harvey, and Michael Finley, January 2000

B7: *Lateral Leadership*: *Getting Things Done When You're NOT the Boss*, Fisher, Roger, and Alan Sharp, August 2004

B8: *Grass Roots Management: How to Grow Initiative and Responsibility in All Your People*, Browning, Guy, Financial Times Management June 2003

APPENDICES

☐

Appendix 1: 6 Principles of HPT Best Practice

1.   Use an existing High Performing Teams Model
Don't just try and make one up as you go along!

2.   Conduct a Team Healthcheck
Assess the team against your HPT model by interviewing team members, customers and sponsors. Seek multiple confirming views and evidence.

3.   Establish Team improvement priorities
In your view, with support from your HPT model, select the most important areas where there are significant team process or practice problems.

4.   Build Team Maturity "Basecamps"
 Try to bring your team to specific team "maturity" basecamps BEFORE moving on to the next thing. Some things are foundational and need to be fixed first.

5.   Some things take longer to fix
Some things may be a simple fix (and a quick win) but others will require you to keep going back over them a number of times to get them established solidly. You need to understand which team processes will take more time and effort!

6.   People and Process are interdependent
It is very difficult to implement any processes with unwilling people. It is just as difficult to be motivated in a team where the processes are non-existent or awful. You need to take an integrated view of people and process.

Appendix 2: 10 Principles of Change Management

1.   Build as much insight and relationship as you can with an individual BEFORE you intervene.

2.   Make appropriate interventions which are relevant to the individual's attitude (e.g. don't ask an opponent to become a champion) and use light touch interventions (e.g. opinion/advice seeking) with those who are negative.

3.   Build on supporters rather than attempting to neutralise opponents however ...

4.   Don't neglect any high-profile opponents – they could derail the change if ignored.

5.   Intervene with those you can influence (which depends on their relationship with you and their openness to the proposed change).

6.   Intervene with those who have influence over others (through their authority or social reputation) and make them champions.

7.   Don't neglect indirect interventions (e.g. Teams and Colleagues) as well as direct (one on one) interventions.

8.   Never stop nurturing supporters otherwise enthusiasm and commitment soon wanes.

9.   Be patient – adoption is often slow to start – if you are confident you are doing the right things then stick with it even if the initial results are not yet apparent.

10.   Finally be creative – sometimes you just need to do something not in the standard playbook!

Appendix 3: 7 Beliefs of High Performing Teams

Beliefs are the fuel which can really energise teams

There is one, often neglected area, which a team needs to address as part of a High Performing Team strategy if it wants to be exceptionally successful - team member beliefs. Here I suggest the seven hidden beliefs of high performing teams are:

1. Clear and Public Accountability
2. Trusted Competency
3. Give and Take
4. Outcome Optimism
5. Total Transparency
6. Work is its own Reward
7. Meaningful Mission Value

See the end of this appendix for more about how the research was validated.

THERE ARE TWO FUNDAMENTAL DIFFERENCES BETWEEN BIOLOGICAL AND HUMAN TEAMS

There are two major differences between biological teams and human teams - intelligence and autonomy. Human teams have vastly superior intelligence to biological teams and much greater potential for member autonomous behaviour. Let's look at each in turn.

THE INTELLIGENCE FACTOR

Vastly superior team member intelligence perhaps surprisingly, does not actually make much difference because the bioteams model is a distributed intelligence model and therefore easily accommodates highly intelligent team members.

What we have to ensure here is that team members know the times where they should apply their own intelligence and the times where consistent and immediate member behaviour is more important. I discuss this in more detail under the development of consistent autonomous team member behaviour in Virtual team execution-three action rules from nature:

http://www.bioteams.com/2005/07/14/virtual_team_execution.html

THE AUTONOMY FACTOR

Autonomy means that human team members can choose what, if any action to take, in response to a given stimulus. More importantly it means they can also choose how quickly to act and with what degree of commitment or force. This is fundamentally different from a biological response.

In almost all biological teams (except for the highly intelligent ones such as groups of primates or dolphins) when a team member receives a certain stimulus they will automatically make a pre-determined response without consideration or delay. In biological teams there is nothing between stimulus and response. In human teams there is something between stimulus and response - free will.

FREE WILL AND BELIEFS IN HUMAN TEAMS

How we will act is influenced by the beliefs we hold
regarding the situation we find ourselves in when we
receive the stimulus. Viktor Frankl expands on this in his
famous book Man's Search for Meaning. [1].

For example, if I do not feel I am being adequately
supported or appreciated by the rest of the team I may
avoid action where there is a perceived risk of my failure.
Alternatively, if I felt strongly supported I might take
higher risk actions. In simple terms - biological teams do
not have to address the issue of the team member
motivation whereas human teams do.

This raises the question of how effective bioteams would
be in an organizational team which is suffering from poor
motivation? In my opinion the answer is not very!
Therefore, I suggest that to be really effective a human
bioteam must also take into account the beliefs and
motivations of its highly intelligent and autonomous
members.

LEARNED OPTIMISM - THE IMPACT OF TEAM BELIEFS ON PERFORMANCE

There is actually relatively little written about the impact
of team member beliefs on overall team performance. One
piece of research which partly addresses this issue is the
unique work on "Learned Optimism" by Professor Martin
Seligman [2]. Dr Seligman is a clinical psychologist who
for the last thirty years has studied the areas of learned
optimism and learned helplessness to help individuals deal
with depression and pessimism in their lives.

A Systematic Guide to
High Performing Teams (HPTs)

As a sub-topic within his research Dr Seligman has explored how optimism and pessimism in team members impacts on the overall team performance. His theory is that optimism is better in individuals and teams because when an optimist encounters a setback they will tend to persevere whereas a pessimist will tend to give up.

In the team context he believes that if you have two teams of broadly equal abilities but one team is optimistic and the other team is pessimistic then the optimistic team will recover better from setbacks.

Dr Seligman goes on to prove this in sport using American baseball and basketball teams. For whole seasons he would track two comparable teams and record and rank their optimism / pessimism by the statements they made in the press after defeats. Optimists tend to explain defeats as 'temporary', 'specific' and 'external' whereas pessimists explain things as 'permanent', 'universal' and 'internal'.

Thus to an optimist a set-back is a temporary thing, in a very narrow area which can be fixed or avoided next time. A pessimist however sees a set-back as a permanent thing, wide in scope which reflects a fundamental weakness or situation which is very difficult to do anything about.

THE BELIEFS OF HIGH PERFORMING TEAMS

I found a useful article, 'How to Inspire Your Team', by Charlie Feld in CIO Magazine which suggests that leaders of high-performing teams need to operate from the following four beliefs to get the best out of their staff - Trust, Hope, Enjoyment and Opportunity.

However, I have found no other research in the public domain which directly looks at the beliefs of the team members of high-performing teams. There is however excellent material on the detailed characteristics and behaviours of high-performing teams - two of the most useful are Hot Groups [3] and Organizing Genius [4].

UNCOVERING THE "HIDDEN BELIEFS" OF HIGH PERFORMING TEAMS

From my own experience of teams and by analysing the material mentioned above I have been able to identify a set of about seven hidden beliefs which seem to repeatedly underpin high performing teams (HPT):

1. CLEAR AND PUBLIC ACCOUNTABILITY

HPT team members believe that every member of the team has a clear and public accountability. Every team member knows what they are being counted on for by the others and what they can count on the others for.

2. TRUSTED COMPETENCY

HPT team members believe that the rest of the team trusts them to know how to do their job properly without being supervised. In a multidisciplinary team this translates into "I know what you have to do and am confident you can do it - how you do it is your business"

3. GIVE AND TAKE

HPT team members believe that if they need help they can ask for it and it will be freely offered. They believe that asking for help, in moderation, actually increases their standing within the team rather than diminishing it. They also believe something is badly wrong if somebody is struggling along and not asking for help or is asking for help but being ignored by the team.

4. OUTCOME OPTIMISM

Perhaps not surprisingly as discussed earlier under "Learned Optimism" HPT team members are confident that they (and they alone) are going to succeed in delivering the mission of the project no matter what.

5. TOTAL TRANSPARENCY

HPT team members expect to be kept appraised in an honest and timely manner of any important issues in the project even if it does not directly affect them. This is part of the dynamic of every member believing they are a team leader and able to contribute beyond their specific functional team member briefs. They also believe they are free to pass opinions about situations they are not directly responsible for and these opinions should be respected and listened to.

6. WORK IS ITS OWN REWARD

HPTs enjoy their work and get a satisfaction from it that goes well beyond the remuneration and even beyond the satisfaction of the results and success that they achieve together. Part of this is the social buzz they enjoy working together with like-minded high performers. They might not work for nothing however the "which project" question is more important one than "how much pay for it?" question.

7. MEANINGFUL MISSION VALUE
HPT team members believe that the mission they are engaged on is significant, important and meaningful. They believe that if they are successful they will have made a fundamental contribution to their organization or even to the greater good. If they saw the project as just 'business as usual' or routine, then their motivation would sag significantly. Part of this is that the task must not seem trivial or easy or "done-it-before". HPT team members also generally feel they are the only people in the organization who could succeed at such a difficult task.

GOOD BELIEFS MAKE A TEAM WORK HARDER

One of the main consequences for a team of a set of beliefs like these seven is that it simply makes them more committed and willing to put in the necessary hours for the project to succeed. For example, if you feel trusted, there is a feeling of shared glory, a sense of meaningful mission and the expectation of success then it is more likely you will do whatever it takes to deliver.

Creating a Bioteams includes identifying your team's beliefs

The first step for an ambitious bioteam is to try to honestly identify the current beliefs your individual team members hold. Next these can be compared with the seven high-performance beliefs above to identify the top team motivational issues. As for all belief situations people can be encouraged to modify their beliefs but in the end of the day new beliefs cannot be mandated.

The most powerful techniques for modifying beliefs are firstly illustrating the consequences of current beliefs and secondly modelling alternative beliefs. Both these tasks are the responsibilities of the senior members of the team and the team members whose beliefs are more in line with HPTs. A team operating bioteam principles in harmony with these kinds of team member beliefs has the potential to operate as an ultra-high-performing team.

SUMMARY OF THE RESEARCH METHOD

The 7 beliefs were filtered from a longer set of potential beliefs suggested from a literature review through organizational surveys.

These surveys validated the top beliefs as below. Clearly the top 4 standout!

1 - Clear and public accountability - 100% agreed
2 - Trusted competency - 100% agreed
3 - Give and take - 100% agreed
4 - Outcome optimism - 100% agreed
5 - Total transparency - 80% agreed
6 - Work is its own reward - 80% agreed
7 - Meaningful mission value - 50% agreed

References

1. Frankl, V., 1984. Man's Search for Meaning, Simon & Schuster

2. Seligman, M., 1990. Learned Optimism - How to change your mind and your life, Free Press

3. Lipman-Blumen, J. & Leavitt, H., 1999. Hot Groups - Seeding them, feeding them and using them to ignite your organization, Oxford University Press

4. Bennis, W., 1997. Organizing Genius - The Secrets of Creative Collaboration, Nicholas Brealey Publishing

☐

Annex to App. 3 – Team Beliefs Questionnaire

TEAM MEMBER BELIEFS QUESTIONNAIRE (Page 1)

Please state to what extent you agree with each of the following statements. You may also make short optional comments. No answers will be attributed to yourself.

Q1. Everybody in my team knows what they can count on me for. (1a)
5=Strongly Agree, 4=Agree, 3= Not Sure, 2=Disagree, 1=Strongly Disagree

Comments

Q2. My team are confident that I have the skills to deliver.   (2a)
5=Strongly Agree, 4=Agree, 3= Not Sure, 2=Disagree, 1=Strongly Disagree

Comments

Q3. My team expect me to ask for help whenever I need it without it having to be imposed.   (3a)
5=Strongly Agree, 4=Agree, 3= Not Sure, 2=Disagree, 1=Strongly Disagree

Comments

Q4. I expect to be kept fully up-to-date on how the project is going and any important news or issues - I don't expect there will be "team secrets" I don't hear about.   (4a)
5=Strongly Agree, 4=Agree, 3= Not Sure, 2=Disagree, 1=Strongly Disagree

Comments

Q5. I expect we will all share the credit or blame for the results we produce - I don't expect the team leaders to take all the glory or pain.
(5a)
5=Strongly Agree, 4=Agree, 3= Not Sure, 2=Disagree, 1=Strongly Disagree

Comments

TEAM MEMBER BELIEFS QUESTIONNAIRE (Page 2)

Q6. I believe what we are doing on this team is really significant – it is one of the most important projects in our organisation.   (6a)
5=Strongly Agree, 4=Agree, 3= Not Sure, 2=Disagree, 1=Strongly Disagree

Comments

Q7. I am confident that my team will deliver the result here.   (7a)
5=Strongly Agree, 4=Agree, 3= Not Sure, 2=Disagree, 1=Strongly Disagree

Comments

Q8. We have to be careful what we say to staff outside the team – it's a 'need to know' basis.   (8a)
5=Strongly Agree, 4=Agree, 3= Not Sure, 2=Disagree, 1=Strongly Disagree

Comments

Q9. Rewards and bonuses are nice but the work and the sense of achievement is really the main thing for me on this team.   (9a)
5=Strongly Agree, 4=Agree, 3= Not Sure, 2=Disagree, 1=Strongly Disagree

Comments

Q10. We are that bit better than the other groups in our organisation and will show off our achievements and abilities wherever we get the chance.   (10a)
5=Strongly Agree, 4=Agree, 3= Not Sure, 2=Disagree, 1=Strongly Disagree

Comments

Q11. I know what I can expect everyone else in my team to deliver. (1b)
5=Strongly Agree, 4=Agree, 3= Not Sure, 2=Disagree, 1=Strongly Disagree

Comments

TEAM MEMBER BELIEFS QUESTIONNAIRE (Page 3)

Q12. I am confident that my team members all have the skills to do
what they need to do.   (2b)
5=Strongly Agree, 4=Agree, 3= Not Sure, 2=Disagree, 1=Strongly Disagree

Comments

Q13. I expect to use a reasonable amount of my team time to help
other team members whenever they need it.   (3b)
5=Strongly Agree, 4=Agree, 3= Not Sure, 2=Disagree, 1=Strongly Disagree

Comments

Q14. My frank comments and suggestions on areas of the team outside
my own specific responsibilities will be sought, welcomed and taken
seriously by other team members.   (4b)
5=Strongly Agree, 4=Agree, 3= Not Sure, 2=Disagree, 1=Strongly Disagree

Comments

Q15. I feel I am as much accountable to the other team members as I
am to the official team leader(s).   (5b)
5=Strongly Agree, 4=Agree, 3= Not Sure, 2=Disagree, 1=Strongly Disagree

Comments

Q16. I believe that the team's objectives are difficult and challenging.
                                                              (6b)
5=Strongly Agree, 4=Agree, 3= Not Sure, 2=Disagree, 1=Strongly Disagree

Comments

Q17. I feel we are a top team and have some of the best people in our
organisation on the team.   (7b)
5=Strongly Agree, 4=Agree, 3= Not Sure, 2=Disagree, 1=Strongly Disagree

Comments

TEAM MEMBER BELIEFS QUESTIONNAIRE (Page 4)

Q18. Not everyone in the organisation wants us to succeed – we have to constantly watch our backs and carefully manage the politics. (8b)
5=Strongly Agree, 4=Agree, 3= Not Sure, 2=Disagree, 1=Strongly Disagree

Comments

Q19. We work whatever hours it takes to get the job done – the work comes first in this one. (9b)
5=Strongly Agree, 4=Agree, 3= Not Sure, 2=Disagree, 1=Strongly Disagree

Comments

Q20. We sometimes break organisational rules – this work is just too important to be held back by bureaucracy, politics or petty administration. (10b)
5=Strongly Agree, 4=Agree, 3= Not Sure, 2=Disagree, 1=Strongly Disagree

Comments

** THIS IS THE FINAL PAGE OF THE QUESTIONNAIRE **

SCORING THE QUESTIONNAIRE RESPONSES

This section is <u>not</u> to be given to the individuals <u>when</u> they are completing the questionnaire. you can, of course, share it with them afterwards if you wish.

The questionnaire probes the team members' views on 10 different possible team member beliefs which have been identified in the literature as often being associated with High-Performing Teams to various degrees.

These 10 beliefs are:
1.   Clear and Public Accountability
2.   Trusted Competency
3.   Give and Take
4.   Total Transparency
5.   Shared Glory
6.   Meaningful Mission Value
7.   Outcome Optimism
8.   Success in Spite of/Common Enemy
9.   Work is its Own Reward
10.   Simply the Best

The questionnaire asks the same question in two different ways about each belief to check the consistency of the answers given. The link between the questions and the 10 beliefs are shown in the reference numbers in brackets at the end of each question.

For example, question 2 and question 12 both refer to belief number 2 – Trusted Competency.

The strongest or weakest held beliefs will be those beliefs where the respondent's answers to both questions correlate.

ANALYSING THE QUESTIONNAIRE RESULTS

Best practice is to aggregate the results for all the team members and then to present this summary back to the team for discussion.

You should not identify or focus on the beliefs of any particular individual however individuals may (or may not) volunteer their own beliefs in these discussions.

You can analyse and discuss the results in many different ways including:

1.   Which beliefs are <u>most common</u> to team members?

This can be used to reinforce a strong sense of team *togetherness*.

2.   Which beliefs is there the <u>most variation</u> within the team?

This can help the team understand and value its *diversity*.

3.   Which beliefs are <u>most absent</u> from the team?

This may not be significant or it may indicate that the team lacks *confidence* in the achievability of its objectives. It can therefore lead in nicely to a collaborative team *healthcheck* as to what might be missing or getting in the way.

If you would like to obtain a free copy of the **Team Beliefs Spreadsheet** please email me at <u>www.dashboardsimulations.com</u>

Appendix 4: Integrated HPT Model Infographic

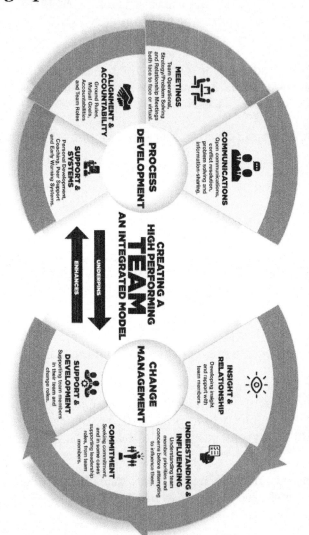

INDEX

A Systematic Guide to
High Performing Teams (HPTs)

Your Own Notes (1)

A Systematic Guide to
High Performing Teams (HPTs)

<u>Your Own Notes (2)</u>

A Systematic Guide to
High Performing Teams (HPTs)

Your Own Notes (3)

Your Own Notes (4)

*A Systematic Guide to
High Performing Teams (HPTs)*

Your Own Notes (5)